# EXPLAINING UNHAPPINESS

## Dissolving the Paradox

PETER SPINOGATTI

iUniverse, Inc.
Bloomington

# Explaining Unhappiness
## Dissolving the Paradox

*The information, ideas, and suggestions in this book are not intended as a substitute for professional advice. Before following any suggestions contained in this book, you should consult your personal physician or mental health professional. Neither the author nor the publisher shall be liable or responsible for any loss or damage allegedly arising as a consequence of your use or application of any information or suggestions in this book.*

*iUniverse books may be ordered through booksellers or by contacting:*

*iUniverse*
*1663 Liberty Drive*
*Bloomington, IN 47403*
*www.iuniverse.com*
*1-800-Authors (1-800-288-4677)*

*Because of the dynamic nature of the Internet, any Web addresses or links contained in this book may have changed since publication and may no longer be valid. The views expressed in this work are solely those of the author and do not necessarily reflect the views of the publisher, and the publisher hereby disclaims any responsibility for them.*

*ISBN: 978-1-4502-5439-7 (pbk)*
*ISBN: 978-1-4502-5440-3 (cloth)*
*ISBN: 978-1-4502-5441-0 (ebk)*

*Excerpts from Equus, written by Peter Schaffer (© 1973), reprinted by permission of Scribner, a division of Simon & Schuster.*

*Direct inquiries may be made to Peter Spinogatti:*
*Telephone: 631 424-0202*
*www.dissolvingunhappiness.com*
*www.explainingunhapipiness.com*
*Email: peterspinogatti@yahoo.com*
*Explainingunhappiness.blogspot.com*

*Library of Congress Control Number: 2010912559*

*Printed in the United States of America*

*iUniverse rev. date: 11/18/10*

FOR PETER

# Contents

# Introduction

*Explaining Unhappiness* is the result of having spent thirty years of my professional life talking to troubled souls and a lifetime of introspection and research. At the risk of appearing immodest, I believe I have written a definitive explanation as to why human beings have always found it necessary to make themselves unhappy. And more important, how this new understanding will allow them to stop doing that.

Serious books inevitably start with an instigating question, and the question that this book answers is, "What are you afraid would happen if you weren't unhappy?" It is not a question of my own making. A former teacher, colleague, and friend asked me that question; it struck me with such force that it eclipsed every other existential question I have ever encountered. Why? Because this is the question that everybody is asking all their lives, without ever fully realizing it. We are also deeply engaged in the assumptions contained within it.

What are we assuming when we ask, "What are you afraid would happen if you weren't unhappy?" First, we're suggesting that it is possible not to be unhappy regardless of the present circumstances in which we find ourselves, that *unhappiness* doesn't just happen, but that it may be self-imposed. Further, this *chosen* state may have less to do with what is happening in the present and more to do with warding off a fearfully anticipated future. Finally, we must also believe that, somehow, unhappiness pays off. We are forced to conclude, then, that we *value* unhappiness, which qualifies as the apogee of human contradiction. It would mean that people who seek help actually value what they hate. They are souls in pain hitting their heads against the wall in their therapists' offices, perversely ignorant that they are choosing to do so, and asking their therapists to treat their headache.

This book is unlike others in the field of self-help psychology. Its pages contain no surveys revealing what groups of people are likelier to be happy, no exercises, quizzes, or personal inventories designed to give readers a deeper understanding of what is wrong with them. It does not offer any steps to self-improvement, realizing your potential, personal growth, or increasing your ability to cope because these traditional goals of therapy assume that there is something about people that has to be put right.

What I am proposing, instead, is that human beings are not defective. I believe that emotional problems—unhappiness, if you will—are produced in a way that might be likened to a person holding his breath. Such a person does not have to be taught how to breathe since his ability to hold his breath would imply that he already knows how to do that. Think of the old joke that goes, "Doctor, it hurts when I do this," raising his arm. To which the doctor replies, "Don't do that." My approach to unhappiness is similarly passive: it seeks change through inaction.

My analysis makes no appeal to religion, mysticism, or the supernatural, not because these approaches to peace of mind are necessarily misguided. In the end, it may well be that the bliss we seek may, indeed, lie with the transcendent. My only interest here is to present a strictly earth–based psychological analysis of human self-definition, and that will only be possible by reexamining human self-consciousness at its foundational level.

A book about happiness should be easy to understand and help people feel better about their lives. It should be inspirational, particularly in its original sense, which means to breathe life into something that is essentially dormant. It should not merely rehash the obvious, stitch together off- the -shelf psychological nostrums, repackage homilies or even offer encouragement instead of reasoned analysis and ultimately fail to satisfy anyone who longs for both. This is not to condemn the genre or those sages who voiced profound insights and fresh perspectives. I hope to be offering you the best of what it should be.

I think we can agree that whatever else happiness may be, it is inextricably bound with knowledge but what do we know now that our philosophic ancestors didn't? What have we learned about grief, anxiety, jealousy, anger, resentment, self-esteem, rejection, and loneliness that might make these issues one jot less painful for us than they were for them? Even Freud believed that psychoanalysis could do little more than replace "hysterical misery" with "everyday unhappiness."

In response to that dismal prognosis, many post-Freudians argued that psychological change wasn't simply a process of building better defenses against threats to one's self-esteem. Real change, they said, must allow for positive growth. The first problem with "growth" is that it is a term borrowed from biology and is simply *declared to exist* in psychology. Biological growth is an observable process because it lends itself to measurable change. In psychology, growth is only a metaphor for change, meaning that rulers and clocks cannot measure it. Nevertheless, *growth* became the buzzword that promised a whole new frame of reference for how we might view ourselves. Who could argue with that?

The second problem with the notion of growth is that it implies that how we see ourselves will always be an unfinished business. Self-doubt will never disappear, and complete self-acceptance will remain forever beyond our reach. Growth, in actual practice, is just another word for "coping"; a new label stuck on the same old bottle. Happiness, on the other hand, is an ongoing, subjective experience of being inwardly peaceful, and that only happens when self-doubt has been removed from our reflections. To anyone who is happy, the idea of growth never comes up. Of course, a happy person can become happier but he is no longer on a mission; he is already where he wants to be

Probably the best example of this knowing state can be found in a spiritual context. Whether it's the Buddha receiving enlightenment under the Bodhi tree or Saul of Tarsus having a conversion experience of the "scales falling from his eyes," it is knowledge of this kind that produces happiness. Whether or not you choose to see these epiphanies as mystically inspired is not at issue here. What matters is the ability to fully experience freedom from self-doubt because that is what reveals our true nature and lies at the heart of what it means to be happy. I hope to show how it is the absence of that freedom that underlies every manifestation of human discontent. Consider, for example, the experience of a mother or father embracing their baby for the first time. Why is such an experience blissful? The answer is that when we love purely, it frees us from even a hint of self-doubt, and all is right with the world because we are right with ourselves.

It is impossible to overstate the importance of self-doubt and its relationship to unhappiness. Historically, self-doubt has always been regarded as an unavoidable feature of the human condition and, to our detriment, viewed as a desirable human attribute. This article of faith found its earliest expression, at least in the West, when Socrates asserted, "I know nothing except the fact of my own ignorance." That statement underpins his entire view of human self-awareness. Socrates convinced self-reflecting human beings that *they* were the problem. Not only did he persuade everyone that "the unexamined life is not worth living" and the "fact" of our problematic consciousness, but that our greatness lay in acknowledging our uncertainty. In effect, he made self-doubt a virtue. It would be difficult to find a philosopher, psychologist or anyone else for that matter who doesn't accept that as the cornerstone of human self-consciousness. As it happens, its unquestioned acceptance has made it impossible for the Greeks and everyone since to resolve the issue of unhappiness. It is a serious error because a system of thought is only as secure as the premise upon which it rests.

This does not mean that a system built on a false premise may not contain individual assertions that are both true and of practical value. Cartographers who drew their maps in the belief that the world was flat did so with sufficient accuracy so as to guide ships to their intended ports. Sailors navigated by the stars in spite of the fact that they believed the earth to be the center of the universe. But when these beliefs produced contradictions and prevented new worlds from being discovered, it became clear that no half-measures would do. Flat-world geographers and geocentric astronomers had to reject their false assumptions, just as we must if we have any hope of becoming happy.

In the modern era, relativism has led philosophers and psychologists to believe that a single idea of happiness cannot have any content. I disagree. Inner peace, self-acceptance, and the like are unquestionably universal features of contentment. The ancient Greeks called this state of mind characterized by freedom from worry or concern *ataraxia*. The message of this book is that there is most assuredly a single idea of unhappiness. Most people view unhappiness not as a strategic construct but rather as a mysterious, negative feeling state materially caused by events inside and outside our bodies over which we have limited control. That belief turns us into victims who now have to be "cured" by others, the control of our unhappiness out of our hands.

It has been said that any scientific approach to the subject of happiness must be able to specify the conditions under which happiness is possible. That, I contend, is bad psychology. Such a point of view presupposes that human happiness is dependent on material conditions rather than the human decision as to how to view those conditions. As the psychiatrist and survivor of Auschwitz, Viktor Frankl, observed, "the last of human freedoms is to choose one's attitude in a given set of circumstances."

# 1

# Unhappiness—
# The Only Psychological Problem

*I have always been impressed by the fact that the most studiously avoided subject of Western philosophy is that of happiness.*

Lin Yutang

*[Neurosis:] ... a mental disorder in which the predominant disturbance is a symptom or group of symptoms that is distressing to the individual and is recognized by him or her as unacceptable and alien.*

Sigmund Freud

What does it mean when someone says they have a psychological problem? A cursory glance would make that appear to be an impossible question to answer because the variety of psychological complaints seems limitless. The ideal answer would be a universally agreed upon definition, some feature or features of human experience that do not depend on any specific cultural or situational considerations for its truth. In a nutshell and at the risk of venturing into an intellectual climate that tends to look at such a question with disfavor, I am contending for what amounts to a psychological absolute.

Anyone who seeks psychotherapy is unhappy. As central to psychotherapy as disease is to medicine, unhappiness still tends to be viewed as too ambiguous to be researched by psychologists and psychiatrists. The logic is that the experience of unhappiness is too subjective, inscrutable even, to be a suitable subject of scientific study. Research psychologists tend to study the behavior of simpler animals instead, and psychiatrists are inclined to classify psychological disorders the same way physicians of other specialties classify physical disorders. In both cases, the main focus is on *observables,* the patient's symptoms are fitted into a psychiatric *disorder* and is then treated with the appropriate drug. The focus on observables is why psychologists tend to study behavior and psychiatrists tend to concentrate on symptoms. The subjective experience of unhappiness—what actually goes on inside us, which is unobservable and the most important part of the phenomenon—gets the least attention. I believe that while it is undeniably true that people who say that they are unhappy may mean different things, the *experience* of unhappiness, at its core, is the same for everyone.

A psychological problem, like all problems, begins with the acknowledgment that there is a problem in the first place, an awareness that something is amiss. We have a mechanical problem when the car fails to start, a medical problem when we break a leg, a financial problem when we lose our job. As it happens, any of these material problems can instantly morph into a psychological problem by simply getting unhappy about their occurrence. Tacking on the phrase "and I am unhappy about that" instantly converts a material problem into an emotional one, and when we do that, it always means that that we are feeling bad. It would be a perversion of language and experience to say you're unhappy if you don't mean you're feeling bad and would prefer not to.

## Feeling Bad as Disorder

Freud's very definition of a "neurotic disorder," as shown above, includes the patient's distress. His was a roundabout way of admitting that only when individuals are feeling bad do they qualify as neurotics. For example, not so long ago mental health professionals were split over the question as to whether homosexuality is a mental disorder. In the first two editions of the *Diagnostic and Statistical Manual of Mental Disorders* (*DSM I* and *DSM II*), it was. After lobbying by, mostly, gay activists, it was decided in *DSM III* that unless "negative societal attitudes toward homosexuality … have been internalized," it was not. More simply, unless a person is feeling bad about his homosexuality, he cannot be said to have a psychological problem.

It is only this subjective element—*people feeling bad*—that can universally define a psychological problem. There are no other reliable objective criteria that can adequately define it, no observable behaviors that are agreed upon by professionals and non-professionals alike that would make a psychological problem more scientifically respectable. This is not the case when abnormal behavior is caused by neurological disorders like Parkinson's, Alzheimer's or paresis. These are bona fide brain diseases with cellular abnormalities that can be objectively confirmed by MRI and PET-scan images.

When no such objective evidence exists, observing abnormal interpersonal behavior becomes an entirely different enterprise. How people behave toward one another is still the place to look, but we now know that labeling something "abnormal behavior" may reveal more about the observer than the observed. What anyone judges as *normal* behavior may be consensually agreed upon, but it is not necessarily desirable. Abraham Maslow was one of the early psychologists to observe that what we refer to as normal may only be the "psychopathology of the average." I prefer to recast that phrase as "ignorance of the average" because pathology is a disease state and suggests that unhappiness might be something that happens to us instead of something we do to ourselves. For many of us, what people do may strike us as idiosyncratic or eccentric and that may be a problem for *us,* but unless those who are being observed are also uncomfortable with their behavior, it need not be a problem for them.

Presumably, the hard evidence for a psychological disorder has developed from the abnormal interpersonal behaviors issuing from a level of self-absorption that includes chronic contempt of or indifference to other people. The extremes of these behaviors range from the antisocial aggression of the sociopath to the asocial hallucinatory withdrawal of the psychotic. Sociopaths are able to kill without remorse, and hallucinating psychotics seem to be more comfortable with the reality only their minds witness. So whether for lack of empathy or of interest, this lack of *feeling* for other people is cited as objective evidence for the existence of a psychological disorder.

## Feeling Bad as Deviance

I am not suggesting that a person who kills without conscience does not have a psychological problem. I am arguing that determining he has a psychological problem by his remorseless killing is not an objective test. If it were, soldiers, parents, and others who kill in the interest of patriotism, protection of loved ones, or in self-defense, who also may not feel bad about it, would also qualify as sociopathic. Clearly, they are not. Sociopaths don't kill for those reasons however. If they kill, it's for sex, money, and power; and they do not feel bad about what satisfies those ends. But that is not to say that they are not troubled human beings. The fact is sociopaths are a resentful, angry, self-contemptuous lot. Their need to dominate clearly indicates that they fear being dominated themselves. They often complain about feeling "hollow" or "empty," and they are incapable of loving. Usually, their worst fear is that their imperfections and weaknesses will be found out. All of which would lead to the conclusion that sociopaths would not be best described as contented human beings who kill people simply as an avocation.

Similarly, when we consider our second instance of grossly unconventional interpersonal behavior, the asocial withdrawal of the psychotic, that withdrawing from society in itself is not conclusive evidence of a psychological disturbance. What makes the reclusiveness of a psychotic different from a hermit's is the reason for his self-imposed isolation. A recluse who is motivated by his fear or hatred of other people is necessarily unhappy; a hermit who seeks God in solitude or the self in Nature may not be.

Then there is the issue of hallucinations that often accompany psychosis. We tend to agree that hallucinatory experience stands in direct opposition to conventional reality testing and impairs our ability to function. Hallucinations are almost the gold standard for the existence of a psychological problem. I heard a joke recently that asked, Why is talking to God called praying, but if God talks to you, it's called schizophrenia? The joke makes an important point. An atheist might say praying to someone who doesn't exist as well as hearing voices in response is hallucinatory. On the other hand, a theist who believes in the power of prayer would call a positive auditory response to it divine revelation. The French heroine Joan of Arc believed that God had spoken directly to her through angels, and so did the countrymen that she led to victory. It hardly impaired her capacity to test reality or her ability to function. That she was later condemned to death, as a heretic, for the same perception is another matter. Moreover, there are cultures that regard hallucinations as a special gift, a form of prescience, and elevate the hallucinator to the position of priest or shaman. We also know that sensory and sleep deprivation, drugs, electric stimulation, hypnosis, and intense desire can induce hallucinations.

No one would suggest that hallucinations induced in these ways indicate a mental disorder.

The only other way hallucinations occur is through what might be characterized as "emotional overloading," which is to say that the hallucinator is experiencing intense negative feelings about something, which causes the hallucination. Often the complaint is about the hallucination itself, but it always involves the presence of bad feelings.

So, we can see that no matter how bizarre, unconventional, or deviant the behavior of others may appear to us, unless the individual feels bad about it or whatever led up to it, no psychological problem can be objectively shown to exist. If there is a tendency to resist a strictly subjective criterion of "feeling bad" to define a psychological problem, the reason has more to do with social engineering than science. It is generally held by those in political and religious authority that no society can afford to leave definitions of what constitutes appropriate feelings and behavior to individuals; it might lead to anarchy and threaten society's survival. For that reason, internecine homicide like human sacrifice, the execution of criminals, as well as ethnic and religious purges can only be sanctioned by the powers that be, and frequently are. To this end, Joan of Arc was convicted by the Court and burnt to death, as a heretic, for the very claims that made her a heroine before her condemnation and ever since, but would also classify her as mentally ill in our time.

Understandably, we tend to resist the prospect of social deviance flourishing outside the mainstream of socially accepted values. It is an important social question and one that was discussed in general terms 2,500 years ago by Plato. He was very much concerned with the possibility of "bad men who live pleasant lives" and the disruptive social impact that unpunished miscreants might have on the state. Although Plato maintained that virtuous men are always happy and bad ones are always miserable, he apparently had his doubts. That doubt is evidenced by his doctrine of the "noble lie," which was a stratagem devised to mask the possibility that a bad citizen might still be a happy person. He believed that under no circumstances should a legislator ever admit that was possible. Only in this way would citizens be discouraged from engaging in uncivil behavior. Plato's interest here was that of a reformer, and he was prepared to lie if it accomplished good social ends. He did not deceive himself into thinking that he was doing anything other than social engineering, which, in this instance, was the Greek propagandistic precursor to "crime doesn't pay." It was as untrue then as it is today because, unfortunately, there will always be those individuals who believe that crime does pay and all too often they are proven right. They are punished neither by society nor themselves. In any case, criminals tend to be viewed as sick or evil, while they are neither; they are unhappy and dangerous. The mistake is to confuse a strategy of social control, however well intentioned—and in the instance of violent crime, necessary—with psychological reality, confounding what ought to be with what is.

I want to underscore that we are always free to dislike social deviance. In order for the state to be viable, it must always be free to constrain such behavior when it is a crime, but deviant behavior, whether deemed so by personal preference or social necessity, can never serve as the objective basis for what constitutes a psychological problem. Only the individual can determine that, and that, I submit, is done by feeling bad.

## Feeling Bad as Denial

Against this subjective criterion, it might be argued that even if we were to accept the notion that other people's judgment of us can never determine the existence of a psychological problem, might we not be mistaken in our judgment of ourselves? Might not people be unaware that they are feeling bad? After all, don't we regularly "lose touch with our feelings"?

This notion of losing touch with one's feelings has become part of the language of psychology. The problem is that it has become a cliché. Like most clichés, it may have begun soundly enough, but instead of being a preliminary observation with limited application, it has tended to calcify into dogma. For instance, there are some people who feel bad and resist admitting it. It has also been observed that when people are encouraged to acknowledge and express their bad feelings, they seem to feel better. In a field where helping people to stop feeling bad is a very difficult thing to do, anything that might help in that regard becomes welcome. But even then, "letting it all hang out" ends up solving nothing. The problem is that simply venting fails to explain why the person was feeling bad in the first place; it ends up producing a never-ending cycle of getting in touch with the bad feelings, ventilating them, and feeling relief—until the next time when the bad feelings arise again, often about the same thing. That is why letting it all hang out is bad therapy. It confounds self-expression with self-knowledge.

The second difficulty with the idea of losing touch with one's feelings is that it presumes that such a phenomenon is common. The opposite is true. It is precisely the fact that people generate bad feelings with such regularity that leads them to seek therapy. The point is that it is impossible to have a psychological problem and not be aware of it. A pain that is not felt is a contradiction in terms; the same is true of unhappiness. The very essence of feeling bad is awareness. In any event, all doubts about how one is feeling can be easily resolved by posing a question: If we could choose our feelings, would we choose these feelings? If the answer is no, then we are feeling bad.[1]

Other than the subjective experience of feeling bad, there are no clinically identifiable features of behavior that would receive universal agreement in describing a psychological problem. Explanations, both natural and supernatural, are as numerous and varied as the cultures where they occur, but at the level of everyday human experience, unhappiness is not culture-specific. Regardless of culture or how they account for it, anyone who claims to have a psychological problem is always aware of feeling bad.

---

1    Another possible response to this question might be a "not feeling bad" state that lies somewhere between unhappy and happy, despair and bliss, a sort of nondescript *okay* feeling, which, although improvable, wouldn't require any therapeutic intervention.

# 2

# "Nobody's Perfect"–The Origin

*What is called good is perfect and what is called bad is just as perfect.*

Walt Whitman

*Mistakes are at the very base of human thought. If we were not provided with the knack of being wrong, we would never get anything done.*

Lewis Thomas

*The perfect do not have to reflect on the details of their actions.*

Thomas Merton

*The solution to the problem is seen as the vanishing of the problem.*

Ludwig Wittgenstein

*The patient comes to the therapist principally because he cannot accept himself.*

Paul Tillich

*They first raise a dust, then complain that they cannot see.*

Bishop Berkeley

*From a contradiction, you can deduce everything.*

Alan Turing

If several thousand years of recorded history have not significantly advanced our capacity to describe human discontent beyond what, in the end, amounts to the experience of feeling bad, it must be due to how we have been instructed to view ourselves. Societies have decreed that human beings are too flawed to be to be trusted as the final judge of their emotional life. After all, nobody is perfect. Right?

Say to anyone with complete seriousness that you believe that they *are* perfect and observe their response. Without exception, that statement is met with nervous laughter, denial, or derision. Nearly everyone accepts the idea of human imperfection as one of the givens of existence. It's a theme that has been espoused and amplified throughout the ages. Plato spoke about man's "imperfect intellect"; Christianity teaches that man is concupiscent, Marx proposed that man's "alienation" was caused by social and economic conditions; Freud stated that consciousness is not perfectly free and cannot be trusted to act rationally; existentialists claim the opposite, that it is precisely man's freedom that produces his resulting anxiety and self-distrust; and B. F. Skinner denied freedom altogether, stating that humankind's maladaptive behavior is due to the "unhappy conditions of the world." The world teaches us that we are flawed, and we accept it without a ripple of protest. Everyone accepts this dismal doctrine and however differently these thinkers may view human nature, they are all in agreement that we are flawed, because, among other reasons, we make mistakes. If perfection is defined as a state of being that is without error, human beings are, indeed, imperfect, because we are fated to make mistakes. Nonetheless, it must be said that erroneous events sometimes turn out to be serendipitous blessings in disguise and have led to impressive artistic, scientific, military, and business achievements.

It is also worth noting that despite our "fallible nature," we really are superb decision makers. We are spectacularly adept at making good choices. Today, for example, we made literally thousands of choices, mostly without notice. The reason they missed notice is that what we wanted seamlessly dovetailed with our expectations. We probably didn't slip on a banana peel, put our toothbrush in our eye instead of our mouth, or close a door on our thumb. We correctly estimated when to step on the brake to avoid the car in front of us, our car brakes being in good working order; when it was safe to smile at the friendly face on the subway; and when to avert our eyes and check our wallets. During the course of a day, a week or even a lifetime, the number of mistakes we make compared to the number of correct choices is miniscule. The number of fine adjustments (choices) the human body is capable of making is astounding. People who make robots know this better than anyone. The prospect of creating a robot capable of duplicating the nuanced dexterity of the human hand is daunting enough. Making an automaton capable of replicating the repertoire of possible behaviors of a complete human being sends the mind reeling. Who but a myopic ingrate would fail to be awed by the perfection of such an exquisitely tuned engine?

Nevertheless, the existence of mistakes as the surest evidence for human imperfection is universally held. The problem with that characterization is that it fails to take into account that unintended outcomes, like all outcomes, are influenced by randomness, as imposed by reality. It is the failure to appreciate the intrinsic unpredictability of natural events that causes this fallacious thinking. In order to demonstrate that randomness is a permanent feature of reality, let's turn to the hard sciences.

## Randomness, Free Will, and Perfection

Physicists, before the advent of quantum mechanics, believed that better methods of observation and experimentation would eventually make it possible to predict the outcome of physical events with perfect certainty. Werner Heisenberg, a leading figure in quantum mechanics, said that was an illusion. His uncertainty principle stated that the very act of observing an event changes what is being observed. This revolutionary discovery showed that although scientists could know the position of a subatomic particle, they could not measure its momentum at the same time, and vice versa. The more you know about one, the less you can know about the other. Uncertainty is forever built into physical events.

In biology, chanciness is also the case. Numerous mutations occur through pure chance, an event known as genetic drift. A mutation is a random process by which natural selection produces a new, identifiable characteristic. Although most mutations are fatal, when a specific trait proves to be adaptable, it ensures the survival of a new species. When it doesn't but still manages to survive, we call it an oddity. That is why long-necked giraffes are considered a species, but conjoined twins are viewed as an anomaly, a "mistake of nature." However, to call such children a mistake is to fail to grasp that conjoined twins, like all natural events, are the product of numerous, random, external and internal variations, which can cause chromosomal damage. Judging natural selection as imperfect because it kills off most of its mutations is as absurd as finding fault with plate tectonics because shifts in the earth's crust cause earthquakes. Natural selection ensures the survival of a species, and plate tectonics maintain the integrity of the earth. The fact that both of these processes cause loss of life and devastation does not make nature any less perfect.

Since randomness is always integral to atoms and genes, it will also be true of all behavior, including human behavior. Are we not composed of atoms and genes, and wouldn't our choices be subject to the same unpredictability? Clearly, human endeavor will always be influenced by random, external and internal changes to which all phenomena are subject. That means mistakes are not proof of imperfection; they are choices made amidst a current of never-ending variables, probability estimates that didn't pan out. Although it is true that the more information we have, the better chances for a preferred outcome, but anyone who literally subscribes to the idea that they would never make a choice until they had "all the facts" would be paralyzed because in the real world, complete knowledge of those facts is impossible.

I don't mean to suggest that people are not responsible for their mistakes. We are, but only in the same way that nature is responsible for mutations and earthquakes. We do not expect nature to stop producing lethal, but necessary events. If nature is not less perfect for producing biological anomalies and geological calamities, how can we, who are also part of nature and who live in that same uncertain world, be any less perfect?

Despite what I hope we can agree is a sound *scientific* case for the unavoidability of randomness in the world of natural events and its influence on outcomes, there are many who would still deny randomness on religious grounds. They do not accept the innate unpredictability of natural events; they deny the reality of accidents. But most theologians tell us that although God is omniscient, he is not a determinist. Their argument runs something like this: If God knows everything, then he knows what will happen in the future. Since he knows what is going to happen and he can't be wrong, then what we choose to do must always be in accord with what he already knows. Therefore, we would be nothing more than marionettes that God created us because he wanted to watch a puppet show. Not even a fatalist would want to worship such a God. I would suggest that even if the events of the world were predestined, the response to them can't be foreordained. The classic "it is written" kind of thinking only refers to the events themselves, separate from any human reaction to them.2 That is why God granted us free will and, in so doing, renounced perfect knowledge of the future. To do otherwise would immutably determine each of our fates and deprive us of control over our own salvation.

And so, like nature, God has also infused the world of human affairs with uncertainty. Viewed through the prism of science or religion, no event is exempt. We are, therefore—whether creatures of God or products of Nature or both—no less perfect because we are subject to the same unpredictability that God or Nature reserve for themselves.

Now if it is true that life is a horse race, and when things don't turn out, it is never because "we should have known better"; if we stop arrogating for ourselves the prescience that neither Nature nor God claim; if, in effect, we completely discredit the argument that fallibility indicates imperfection, could this knowledge be enough to make us happy? Certainly, we would continue to hold ourselves responsible for unintended outcomes, but that is a far cry from condemning others and ourselves because we consider mistakes as evidence that there is something wrong with us. It would change how we see ourselves, because we will have removed blame and self-doubt from our psychological landscape. If fallibility has been the only measure of imperfection, then eliminating it would restore us to a perfect state. How can one improve on that? The answer is you can't. I don't mean this as a semantic joke—perfection by definition not improvable—but rather, to strike a more profound note: the very nature of negative self-reference makes improvement impossible.

## The Liar's Paradox

We know what is supposed to happen when we improve our financial status or golf score. But just what is supposed to happen when we improve the self? Simply put, the improved self would be one that had eliminated self-doubt and brought self-acceptance. These are the elements of self-esteem. If we were to search for a single explanation of human unhappiness, nothing would better describe it than low self-esteem. It lies at the heart of all discontent. Low self-esteem and personal happiness cannot co-exist.

To understand how widespread the problem of low self-esteem is, just scan the media. It is neither accidental nor incidental that the largest

---

2   In all of Western literature, no greater illustration of this truth can be found than in the Book of Job in the Old Testament. Job, despite the fact that he is a truly good man, is beset by unspeakable calamities but still will not be deflected from his love of God.

and most frequented section in most bookstores is the self-improvement aisle. In addition, most consumer advertising targets a population who perceive themselves to be deficient and needy. We're not pretty enough, not smart enough, not thin enough, not free enough, not successful enough. That's the real reason we need all those services, products and books. Even psychotherapy, which ostensibly addresses a host of psychological problems—anxiety, depression, addictions, relational issues—keeps coming back to this central question: the problem of low self-esteem. It is important to understand that low self-esteem is not simply an attribute of unhappiness; it is its sine qua non. As theologian Paul Tillich reminded us, "The patient comes to the therapist principally because he cannot accept himself."

To use a medical analogy, we might compare low self-esteem to a defective immune system, which makes possible all types of diseases and infections. Similarly, low self-esteem is systemic in that it makes possible all manner of negative emotional states. Should we treat all these complaints as separate problems or tackle the source without which none of these complaints would have emerged in the first place? Clearly, the latter is the only rational choice. The question then becomes how do we attain self-esteem? One way we can solve the problem is to add to ourselves the things that are missing, as we might take a medicine to battle a disease. The other way would be to reject the idea of imperfection altogether, in which case self-improvement would be unnecessary and no medicine would be needed. If people did not put themselves down, there would be no need to lift them back up.

To be sure, people who seek self-improvement to address their low self-esteem, in and out of therapy, produce disappointing results. Why their condition doesn't change may be explained in a variety of ways. It is generally agreed that among the most resistant behaviors to change are the so-called "addictions." On the most superficial level, the explanation for such intransigence may be that the addict has not really decided to change. Instead, he believes that, on balance, his not changing may not be all that self-defeating. For example, smokers may believe that they will still have enough time to stop before they cause irreparable damage. Or they may believe that, despite the increased risk, the odds are still safe enough that they won't get a disease. In other words, while they might agree they *should* change, they are not entirely convinced that it's necessary to alter their behavior. On the other hand, if a smoker knew with absolute certainty that one more cigarette would kill her, would her urge to smoke continue to be "irresistible"?

The primary reason for resistance to change, however, has nothing to do with lack of commitment. Take the dieter. A 95 percent failure rate is the reported number for this group. Although the immediate purpose is to lose weight, the ultimate objective is self-acceptance. At that point, the dietary problem also becomes a psychological problem. But even among those who succeed in losing weight, any improvement in their self-esteem still seems ephemeral. What generally happens is that the whole enterprise of self-improvement is aborted, which becomes one more reason for the dieter to dislike herself, or she succeeds in accomplishing her stated objective, only to find that she still isn't satisfied.

A client once told me "If I passed my reflection, I'd cry. I combed my hair to hide my moon face; new clothes made me cry." Over many years, she would succeed in losing weight and then gain it back. "I'd say to hell with it. I'm tired of feeling deprived all the time," she confided. As a veteran dieter, she was fully aware of all the rehashed explanations for people's failure to lose weight. She heard everything from the familiar— that her weight was a strategy for avoiding intimacy, which is already a comment about lack of self-esteem—to the downright silly—that she had a latent death wish. (Serious suicides do not try to kill themselves by the inexpedient process of clogging their arteries.)

Of course, not every dieter succumbs to such discouragement and there are those who succeed in losing weight; but even then, why does becoming thinner not achieve our dieter's ultimate objective, which is self-acceptance? In spite of her experience with all kinds of therapy, despite all the help she sought and all the diets she'd tried, she could not rid herself of the suspicion that losing weight wasn't going to entirely solve her problem. She believed that at best she'd be thin but still unacceptable, that despite all her efforts at self-improvement, she still could not be trusted to like herself.

In nearly every case, successful dieters may learn to take "only a taste," reformed wife-beaters learn to work off aggression, agoraphobics may learn to travel, but residuals of the addiction remain in the form of qualms about the condition of the plane or quitting smoking but getting fat. It's the same reason that many sober alcoholics become "chocoholics" when they go on the wagon. Although an addiction to chocolate represents a clear improvement over an addiction to vodka, the issue of self-suspicion remains unresolved. It's also the reason why alcoholics who quit drinking must avoid happy hour. As a matter of policy, Alcoholics Anonymous requires that alcoholics never stop viewing themselves as out of the woods. And so the need to improve ourselves becomes an endless merry-go-round that ensures our unhappiness. Regardless of the improvement, self-esteem always seems to remain an unfinished business; self-doubt never disappears. On the other hand, when change is not associated with self-esteem, change flows naturally.

My uncle, an unassuming former farmer, smoked heavily for thirty years. One day I happened to notice that he was not smoking, and asked if he had stopped. He told me that he had and went on to speak of other things. But his easy dismissal of a habit he had enjoyed for so many years intrigued me. I asked him if he'd found it hard to quit. My question appeared to confuse him. At first, I thought it was a language barrier. He had emigrated from Italy several years earlier via Venezuela and his English was not on a par with his native Italian or his adopted Spanish. Believing that I had been misunderstood, I asked him again if he found it difficult to give up tobacco. He only repeated that he had stopped. When I asked him why he had stopped, he said he really wasn't sure. It had simply occurred to him that he didn't want to smoke anymore, and he never thought about it again.

I realized that the issue of how he viewed himself never entered into his decision. Notions such as "addiction," "willpower," "self discipline" and "withdrawal" would have sounded like so much psychobabble. He didn't want to smoke anymore, so he didn't. It had nothing to do with how he saw himself. I have encountered any number of people who acted in a similar way. I had a client who was a mainline heroin addict. He decided one morning that he "simply had enough of it" and stopped. He told me he never even experienced withdrawal symptoms. I have known people who walked away from unsatisfactory professions and relationships and never looked back. As long as changing behavior is unrelated to self-esteem, change follows naturally. Conversely, the desire to change when esteem-driven, even when successful, the suspect consciousness would continue to be suspect and inevitably lead to other self-defeating behaviors.

Then what can we do to solve the problem of self-esteem? The answer is nothing. If the problem of self-esteem has not been solved, it is because it is intrinsically unsolvable. Self-esteem cannot be solved by anything we do; it can only be dissolved by *not doing*. In order to clarify the futility of the self-improvement enterprise, it might be useful to relate the following dialogue that a client (Self-deprecator) had with me (PS). This conversation might have begun with any number of put-downs: "I'm not really into people"; "I'm not fun to be with"; "I'm not smart enough"; "I'm too fat." Bear in mind that how ever the presenting complaints differ, self-doubt and not knowing what to do about their unhappiness is always in the mix. Hence the first line in our dialogue:

Self-deprecator: I feel stupid.

PS: What would you have to know to get smart?

Self-deprecator: If I knew that, I wouldn't be stupid.

PS: If you're too stupid to know how to get smart, wouldn't that also mean you were not smart enough to know that you're stupid?

Self-deprecator: Are you saying I'm stupid to believe I'm stupid?

PS: No, I'm saying that once you call yourself stupid you call into question your ability to ever recognize anything that will allow you to like yourself.

Self-deprecator: I spent my whole life trying to like myself and failed. Of course, I'm stupid.

PS: You are only ignorant, not stupid.

Self-deprecator: What's the difference?

PS: Ignorance is simply the acknowledgement that you don't know something. It is temporary and remediable. Stupidity is permanent and incorrigible.

Self-deprecator: Okay, I'll go along. How do I stop believing I'm stupid?

PS: You might ask yourself what you'd be afraid would happen if you stopped believing you were stupid?

Self-deprecator: I am afraid I would remain stupid.

PS: Why do you believe you would *remain* stupid if you didn't believe that you *were* stupid?

Self-deprecator: These questions aren't helping.

PS: What questions do you think might help?

Self-deprecator: How am I supposed to know? You're the expert.

PS:   If you know that my questions aren't helping, I should think there must be some basis for rejecting them. Do you know what that might be?

Self-deprecator: I don't, but I can spot a good question when I hear it.

PS:   Are you sure you haven't heard the right ones already? After all, you claim to be stupid.

Self-deprecator: Your questions just create other questions.

PS:   Why is that?

Self-deprecator: I don't know. This is all so confusing. I just feel stupid.

As you can see, self-deprecators return to where they began. They trust themselves to know they have a problem but cannot trust themselves to know how to solve it. They believe they are smart enough to know that they are stupid, but they also believe that they are too stupid to know how to get smart. They disqualify themselves as judges and then proceed to sit in judgment of themselves. The self-deprecator perceives himself as both deceivable and deceptive, an unregenerate object of self-suspicion. In a word, the self-deprecator suspects that he is a liar. Who among us has not prefaced a remark with "I know I could be kidding myself, but …" Self-doubt, which always co-exists with low self-esteem, means that we cannot be trusted to know what is true. It embroils us in what philosophers call the Liar's Paradox: "I am a liar" is a statement whose truth leads to a contradiction and whose denial also leads to a contradiction. If I call myself a liar, and that statement is true, then by virtue of the fact that I just told the truth, I cannot be a liar. The statement is false. But if I really am a liar, then the statement "I am a Liar" must also be a lie and therefore true. In other words, if the statement is true, then it is false. If it is false, then it is true.

A great deal of intellectual energy has gone into trying to solve this problem, because paradoxes are intimately connected with some of the deepest and most important ideas in philosophy, logic, and mathematics. Bertrand Russell, one of the most prominent philosophers of the twentieth century dealing with paradoxes of self-reference, showed that there is no way of solving self-referential paradoxes. A set cannot include itself as a member of that set and not lead to a vicious circle and nonsense. The only way to deal with a paradox is to banish it. In other words, you don't solve a paradox: you dissolve it.

It follows then that the resolution to the Liar's Paradox points to the resolution for self-esteem and unhappiness. When anyone believes that they may be a liar, can they ever know if what they are saying is true or false? You can see it is impossible to negatively refer to oneself and not produce the same circular result. People who refer to themselves negatively are also embroiled in a paradox or contradiction, but in this case, it is a *felt* contradiction. In psychological terms, it is the disagreeable experience known as "cognitive dissonance," a phrase coined by the psychologist Leon Festinger.

Recent split-brain research has confirmed that belief formation always avoids the contradictory. Compare the brain to the computer. All modern computers use a binary numerical system, which means they use only two symbols, typically "1" and "0" in endless combinations. It is an either/or, hardwired system, which is to say a symbol must be either 1 *or* 0 but never both. If this rule were violated, the computer would crash. But let's imagine for the moment that it didn't and imagine further that it had feelings; what would the experience of 1 *and* 0 be like?

The answer might best be answered by the Danish philosopher Soren Kierkergaard, who had a lot to say about this either/or kind of thinking. He said, "Either/or is the road to heaven, both/and is the road to hell." And although he was talking about two different views of life, I am suggesting that "both/and" kind of thinking is equally hellacious in the context of negative self-reference.

This is not to say that both/and kind of thinking is necessarily a mistake in other areas of human endeavor, but when applied to oneself, both/and is always the road to hell. Either we can be trusted to tell the truth or we can't. The both/and is the double-bind experience of holding two beliefs that are at odds with one another. It is the essence of inner conflict, a little like arm wrestling with oneself and believing that one arm can win without the other losing; it is the disquieting experience of a person trying to enjoy a cigarette while simultaneously contemplating the prospect of contracting lung cancer, or the experience of eating a sirloin steak and at the same time worrying about clogging one's arteries.

The way out of this dilemma is to understand that contradictions are illusory. Nature doesn't produce contradictions (it is not Nature's responsibility that we fail to comprehend Her). When we are confronted with a contradiction, it is the result of having made a mistaken assumption—often unconsciously embedded in language which filters how we observe and describe Her—that unwittingly limits and distorts our understanding.

And we, who are also part of nature, make the same error when we, through a similarly distorted lens, observe ourselves. The mistaken assumption is that it is possible to solve a problem when the problem is the problem-solver himself, that a self who defines itself as untrustworthy can engage in a program of self-improvement and achieve self-esteem. Self-esteem will not be realized by doing, but by *not* doing. This is not a new idea. Even without the benefit and support of modern logical analysis, a great sage discovered the notion of dissolution long ago.

## Wu Wei, the Path of *Not* Doing

Lao Tzu, the founder of Taoism, wrote 2,500 years ago, "Because the sage is able to forget his self, therefore his self is realized." His philosophy of *wu wei* translates roughly as *not doing*. It is the ancient equivalent of getting out of your own way. Bishop Berkley's observation, "First they make a dust, then complain that they can't see," seems an apt metaphor in this regard. Unfortunately, the idea of *not* making a dust—of wu wei—is not known to most people. It is especially alien in the West, where success is always gauged by taking an action. That is why we continually seek to improve ourselves by adding what we believe is missing.

Although the idea of flawed human nature can be found in virtually every known civilization, the philosophers of ancient Greece explored the question with a zeal unknown until that time. When Socrates stated that "the unexamined life was not worth living" and Plato asserted that man's greatness lay in the acknowledgment of his "imperfect intellect," they were setting the philosophic cornerstone that unwittingly ensured the existence of unhappiness, the very problem they were trying to solve. They did not realize that the rational Greek mind, which was encouraged to doubt everything, must never doubt the doubter if it hoped to escape the quagmire of paradox and felt contradiction. As Einstein would say, that is an axiom to ignore.

The axiom to be discarded, of course, is that fallibility is proof of human imperfection. It is neither a scientific fact, nor an eternal verity, nor an innocuous concession to modesty. To err may indeed be human, but to forgive may not be divine after all, just simply unnecessary. In sum, human nature *is* to be trusted, and the problem of low self-esteem is not to be solved but dissolved.

# 3

# Unsatisfied Desires–A Matter of Inconvenience

*We would readily express our gratitude to any philosophical or psychological theory which was able to inform us of the meaning of feelings of pleasure and unpleasure.*

Sigmund Freud

*In this world there are only two tragedies. One is not getting what you want, and the other is getting it.*

Oscar Wilde

In the last chapter, we dealt with the belief in flawed human nature and its relationship to unhappiness. Now we need to consider another aspect of the problem of unhappiness. Even perfect people will have desires that continue to go unsatisfied. Whenever people do not get what they want, their response usually signals unhappiness. Offhand, that doesn't seem to be a self-esteem issue. Frustrated desire would appear to be a separate question and as significant in the determination of negative emotional states as low self-esteem.

All of us know the disappointment of wanting something very badly and making every effort to attain it, only to see our prayers go unanswered and our desires unsatisfied. On the other hand, most of us are also aware of the warning, "Be careful what you wish for, you just might get it." On the surface, such advice seems to imply either that people are happier when they don't get what they want, which is an obvious absurdity, or that what people think they want and what they really want may be two different things.

Philosophers and psychologists have long wrestled with the issue of unsatisfied desire and its relationship to human discontentment. Whether we speak of an unrequited love, an unfulfilled ambition, or an unrealized dream, no analysis of human unhappiness would be complete without addressing the fundamental question of how our desires influence our happiness. If all the things we wanted were assigned an equal value, our contentment could be calculated by a simple formula. An individual's level of personal happiness could be estimated by the ratio of satisfied desires to the total number of desires:

$$\frac{\text{SATISFIED DESIRES}}{\text{NUMBER OF DESIRES}} = \text{HAPPINESS}$$

Theoretically, if each of us had a total of ten satisfied desires in the numerator and a total of ten desires in the denominator, we would be perfectly happy (10 ÷ 10 = 1). If we had no satisfied desires in the numerator (0 ÷ 10 = 0), we would be perfectly unhappy. Life in the real world, however, will always contain numerators between a figure more than zero and less than the total number of desires. In short, we will always get some of what we want, but we will never get everything that we want. All of Western and Eastern philosophy has held that since there will always be unsatisfied desires, unhappiness will always be a fact of human life. The best we can do, accepting this analysis, is either to expand the numerator or reduce the denominator. In order to minimize disappointment in our lives, we must satisfy as many of our desires as possible or desire as little as possible. The first approach is generally known as hedonism, the second is stoicism, the ultimate stage of which is *desirelessness*. The logic is impeccable as long as we assume that unsatisfied desire, per se, is the cause of unhappiness.

The problem is that people don't always get unhappy when they don't get what they want. Some unsatisfied desires appear to make us unhappy, while others do not. This would imply that desires are not equal, that there may be some natural hierarchy of desires, the most potent of which, when unsatisfied, lead to unhappiness. The other possibility, of course, is that each of us orders our own desires according to our own priorities. When the most important of these desires fail to be satisfied, unhappiness results. In that event, we would want to know why an individual orders his or her desires in a particular way and then becomes unhappy when they're not satisfied.

## Hierarchy of Needs and Prioritizing

Traditionally, any analysis of the possible hierarchy of human desires begins with biological considerations and the notion of *"need."* Obviously, to make sense, need requires some object, such as food or sleep. In its biological context our biological needs are always determined by survival. "Need" is valued as a motivational construct because it is rooted in identifiable states of physiological tension. Biological needs have the advantage of providing us with a physical basis for a good deal of human behavior. Most often, in an affluent society, we eat, sleep, and satisfy a host of bodily needs without notice or special effort. Hunger, which is usually used as the paradigm for biological needs, is a tissue- deficiency state, the presence of which is made known by a tension in our stomachs. It is that physiological prompting that translates (when we bother to do so) into language; "I'm hungry" being the way we express as our need or desire for "I need" or "I want" food.

These physical sensations become especially urgent when we are unsure of getting what we need. To a starving person, getting food becomes an overriding conscious preoccupation. Extreme states of privation can produce hallucinations of the needed object—optical illusions known as mirages. A man dying in the desert sees a green and watery oasis; a starving woman sees a loaf of bread where there is only a stone. The human organism naturally mobilizes all its instinctual efforts to get what it needs for survival. When survival is not at stake, and it generally is not for most readers of this book, our desire for something may serve a different purpose.

A gourmet's desire for food may start with a sensation in the stomach, but that sensation is generally not perceived as a deficiency state but rather as a welcome opportunity for gastronomic delight. His biological need for food may be served simultaneously, but that plays no part in his conscious motivation. He eats because he loves the taste of food, not because he requires nutrition. Still others, who have neither survival nor a pleased palate as a motive, may see food essentially as fuel; they eat because they want to be able to do other things, and staying hungry distracts them from or interferes with those other things. And finally, for some, the hunger signal is ignored altogether. The anorectic, the religious faster, and the hunger striker renounce their biological needs because it is seen as interfering with their respective ideals of thinness, holiness, and freedom. So great is their ability to prioritize, they are even free to starve themselves to death in the interest of their particular cause. The religious martyr may choose to starve herself not because she wishes to die, but because she has an ideal that is more important than life. If there is a God who rewards sacrifice, then the martyr has made the greatest sacrifice, and for that, she will receive the greatest reward. In traditional religious terms, that means eternal bliss with God. For political martyrs, the rewards are more immediate and earthbound. It may be the belief that one's death will lead to social or political good. In either case, the desired object, death, represents that which is good, and the martyr believes he or she is good for having chosen it.

Except in the case of extreme privation, the conscious motivation for eating is never for survival. Biological need only explains how we would die without nutrition, not why we want food. Stomach pangs are not motives; they signal but do not compel. They get our attention, but they can't force us to eat. If needs for survival can be deferred, ignored, and otherwise prioritized, that must be true of all desires, and unhappiness cannot be the automatic result of an unsatisfied desire in some preexisting hierarchy of human needs. We're not unhappy because of not getting our *stated* want, but rather because of the *unstated* want and our not getting that.

## What Does Anyone Really Want?

In order to answer this question, we need to know what it is that people mean when *they say* they want something. On the most superficial level, that is easy to specify. We want friends, houses, vacations, cars—all sorts of things. But things are never wanted simply for themselves. Except for survival, the objects of our desire are always means to other psychological ends. The clearest example of this means–ends relationship is money. It was invented purely as a medium of exchange, and since it has no intrinsic value as pure means, the psychological ends that money serves are virtually limitless. People want money because they believe it will bring them power, survival, independence, leisure, approval, love, security, status, self-respect, and so forth. Everyone who says they are unhappy because they lack money tell us practically nothing. We need to go further in order to discover what desires are really being frustrated.

At this level of analysis, the task gets more complicated. As we move away from the observable objects of our desires and focus on the psychological ends that these objects serve, we enter an inner subjective world where our motives for wanting money become more obscure. Money may be sought as a means to power, for example, but discovering that much raises even more questions. Is it power for yourself? Is it power over others? Is it both? If for yourself, what does that mean? If over others, power over them to do what—love you, respect you, leave you alone, obey you? Suppose you understood that your desire for money existed because you believed that money had the power to buy you love, then you would be confronted with still another question: Is the desire for power reducible to the desire for love? If every desire is potentially desired for something else, couldn't the questions go on indefinitely? Of course, we could get around this infinite reduction by simply acknowledging that at any given time more than one desire is being served, but that prompts another question: can all these desires peacefully coexist?

Psychoanalysts have pointed out the ambivalent nature of human desire. Some have insisted that every strong desire contains the latent core of its opposite. Gratifying the desire for love, for instance, might frustrate the desire for independence. That is what might be behind the fear of commitment. The desire for security can subvert our desire for enterprise. That accounts for why many people do not go into business for themselves. The desire for fame would undermine our desire for privacy, a problem often experienced by celebrities. If desires are multiple, ambivalent, and not completely knowable, then we can never settle the question of what we really want. We would be in the intolerable position of feeling that we were not getting what we wanted and never knowing for sure just what it was that we weren't really getting.

Fortunately, there is a way out. What we need is a master motive, a psychological aim that all our other wants subserve, a motive that is an end in itself because it is so recognizably at the heart of everything we want. The Latin expression for this ancient Greek idea is *terminus ad quem,* which means the limit or destination point for which we do other things. The reigning motive that will satisfy this requirement is our desire to be happy. Nothing we do ever deviates from that ultimate objective. For instance, what might we say that the desires for power, love, status, and independence share as a common aim? Satisfying any of these desires produces *feelings* of power, love, status, or independence—good feelings. Obviously, the psychological doctrine being invoked here is the pleasure principle. What it says is that we gravitate to things that are satisfying or rewarding and avoid what threatens not to be. Terms like satisfaction, reward, pleasure, and happiness all refer to the experience of feeling good. Nobody denies the power of psychological hedonism to explain most human behavior.

Those who object to psychological hedonism as a master motive only quarrel as to its ability to account for *all* motivation. They would argue that there are other behaviors engaged in for their own sake other than our desire to feel good. We are all familiar, for example, with the notion of "duty for duty's sake" and a whole family of related concepts such as "honor for honor's sake," "love for love's sake."

"Duty for duty's sake" was posited by Immanuel Kant. Among the leading Western philosophers, he alone believed neither happiness nor pleasure to be the ultimate aim of human life. But even Kant never claimed that happiness is not what we naturally want. He only claimed that the business of moral philosophy could not be based on what we naturally want but rather on what we ought to want. Unlike all of the other moral philosophers, Kant's position was that moral behavior must never be motivated by such natural inclinations as the desire to be happy. In other words, if we derive any pleasure from doing our duty, then we are not truly moral, we are not truly good. "Duty for duty's sake," he insisted, must be the product of disinterested reason, separate and apart from our desires and feelings. Kant's mistake is that "disinterested reason" fails completely as a way of accounting for any recognizable human experience. Not even reason can exist unless it satisfies human desire. The pleasure inherent in the most rational of human cognitive activities like mathematics is renown. Great mathematicians speak of the "elegance" of mathematics in ways that often border on the mystical. So, whenever the expression "for its own sake" refers to a psychological aim other than that of happiness or pleasure, the term is misapplied. Reason, duty, honor, love—when attained, all these produce feelings of being rational, dutiful, honorable, and lovable. And all these feelings serve the same master—happiness.

## Pleasure and Pain

The first commonly held belief about pain is that it is the opposite of pleasure. It is not. The misconception is based on the belief that pain is a *primary* sensation like seeing, hearing, tasting, touching, and smelling. On the contrary, both pain and pleasure have to do with *judgment*, not sensation.

This is not to say that pain is unreal or that it exists in some neurophysiologic vacuum; the experience of pain is more complex. To be sure, there are mechanical and chemical changes that take place in various tissues in the body. An unusual pattern of activity appears in the stressed area, but there are no specialized nerves that convey pain in the same way that there are specialized nerves conveying sensations like touch, taste, and smell, for example. The same nerves that transmit ordinary sensations signal the experience of pain. What changes ordinary sensations into painful experiences is exactly what transforms ordinary sensations into pleasurable ones—our judgment of them or more precisely our judgment of ourselves in relation to them. Pain combined with how we see ourselves determines its intensity.

A phenomenon that has been called the "Anzio effect" is worth mentioning in this regard. Anzio was a beachhead in Italy that was taken by American soldiers during World War II. It was observed by medical personnel at the time that soldiers who sustained wounds similar to those of civilians required significantly less morphine than the civilians did. The reason for this was that the soldiers perceived their wounds as a ticket back home, while the civilians experienced their injuries as pointless suffering. Another example: consider the intense pain of a kidney stone, which is sometimes compared to that of childbirth. I once asked my urologist who was treating me for my stone if he had ever asked any of his similarly afflicted female patients, who had also given birth, to evaluate the pain level of both experiences. He said he had, and they unhesitatingly answered "stone." The pain of childbirth is perceived differently than that of a kidney stone because a child passing out of the body represents new life and all the satisfactions associated with that event. On the other hand, a kidney stone passing out of the body is an inert bit of calcium that, for most, represents agonizingly meaningless suffering.

I believe that pain is experienced by most people not only as pointless suffering but also as punishment. How else can we explain why people who are in pain so often ask, "Why me?" In fact, the etymological derivation of the word "pain" in both Greek and Latin is "punishment." Put another way, when bad things happen to good people, the sufferers don't really believe they are good. If they did, they would not blame God or Fate for what befell them. "Why me?" is a paranoid exclamation borne of the suspicion that they are being accused of being bad, that they'd been singled out for some special punishment. If we accepted the fact that randomness was a permanent feature of reality, then the response to any calamitous event would instantly leap up at us, "Why anybody?"

Even if we saw events as preordained, we would still not be prevented from using them as opportunities or, for that matter, benedictions. Victor Frankl observed in the concentration camp where he was imprisoned that inmates who spent their time helping others were more cheerful and survived longer. When misfortune and pain are imbued with intense religious meaning, the results can be awesome. Saints and mystics have been tortured and burned at the stake with no visible signs of discomfort. They welcomed their pain as an opportunity for greater holiness, dismissed it as irrelevant, or even experienced it as joy. A stunning example is the case of Blanche Gamond, a persecuted Huguenot under Louis XIV who wrote, "I received the greatest consolation that I have ever received in my life, since I had the honor of being whipped in the honor of Christ and, in addition, of being crowned with his mercy and consolation ... [when I heard them say] 'We must double our blows; she does not feel them, for she neither speaks or cries' ... And how should I have cried, since I was swooning with happiness from within." [3] On a more personal note, my oldest and closest friend, who was the wisest and most fearless man I was ever privileged to know and who was neither a saint nor a masochist, told me that he regarded pain "as an adventure."

In sum, although pain generally originates as sentience (an awareness of a feeling in the body), the intensity of its impact is the result of self-deprecating judgments. Seen in this light, it is not difficult to understand why small injuries can evoke intolerable pain and why catastrophic ones can evoke none, and why hypnosis and placebos can create analgesia—an insensitivity to pain—without losing consciousness. When self-deprecation is not associated with sensations or feelings, when self-suspicion is not at play, pain is a qualitatively different experience. It can become an experience of pure sensation, and when pure sensation is desired, it can qualify as pleasure.

## Ascetics and Masochists

Understood in this way, "pleasure in pain" cease to be a contradiction and explains why those who actively pursue pain, like ascetics and masochists, experience pleasure in pain. An ascetic consciously denies or ignores what he regards as the lower pleasures of the body because he seeks higher spiritual rewards. Historically, religious self-flagellants mortify the flesh with this single objective in mind. That reward may be called enlightenment, redemption, or purification, but how ever it is expressed, the ascetic wants to believe that he is good. This is equivalent to saying that he wants to feel *good*.

But why do masochists experience pain as the prerequisite to pleasure? For essentially the same reason that their religious counterparts do. However, masochists are appeasing more secular gods. Like ascetics, they believe they

3　Excerpted from *Varieties of Religious Experience*, the classic work on the psychology of religion by William James.

are unacceptable as they are and that their openness to being hurt will earn them the right to feel worthy. But whereas the ascetic experiences joy and exaltation of the spirit through mortification of the flesh, the masochist suffers physical pain for worldly rewards. Pain represents acceptance through self-deprecation and the masochist's search for pain, like the ascetic, is also motivated by the desire to become acceptable. One seeks humility, the other humiliation; both seek worthiness. Neither deviates from the desire to be happy.

If everything we want in life, including pain, is guided by an overarching desire to serve our happiness, it follows then that making ourselves unhappy when we fail to get what we want serves that same end. We have already shown that failing to get what we want does not, in itself, cause unhappiness. So how did the belief that unsatisfied desires make us unhappy come about? Like many beliefs, they start in childhood. Anyone who has children or can remember their own childhood has observed that when children don't get what they want, they pout, cry crocodile tears, throw tantrums, and generally carry on. Such behavior is a deliberate, manipulative act. Showing parents their unhappiness over not getting what they want can prove a very effective method to get Mom and Dad to give it to them. But at some point—and this is important—a transition takes place.

What started as a ploy starts to feel like unbidden unhappiness. We make a leap from what began as a tactic to the full-blown feeling that what we want is what we need. Somewhere during our development, each and every one of us comes to believe that not only is unhappiness an effective method to get others to give us what we want, but that by becoming unhappy, it can also be effective in getting us to give ourselves what we want. Recall anything that you have ever wanted, did not get, and proceeded to get unhappy about. Now ask yourself the following question: What do I think it would mean if I didn't feel bad about not getting what I want? Everyone to whom I've put that question gives essentially the same reply: *I wouldn't care enough to want it anymore, and I would end up not getting it.*

## Ego-Deficient Wanting and Object-Oriented Wanting

We believe that we cannot be trusted to get what we want otherwise. It is this ego-deficient frame of mind that makes us unhappy when we don't get what we want, not the fact that we did not or might not satisfy our desires. That is what sets us up for future disappointment. Moreover, for anyone with that mindset, the experience of getting what we want feels less like joy than relief. By contrast, it is a fundamentally different experience when we are genuinely object-oriented. When we want things because they interest, fascinate, and amaze us, it feels like joy because our ego doesn't have a stake in the outcome As Einstein said, "A person first starts to live when he can live outside himself."

It is the failure to fully appreciate the difference between wanting something because it intrigues us and wanting something because we have something to prove, along with the fact that most people operate from the ego-deficient perspective that has obscured why some people get unhappy when they do not get what they want and others don't. The failure to make the distinction between ego-oriented and object-oriented pursuits has led thinkers to treat objects of human desire as if they had an inherent capacity to make us unhappy. It also explains why sages have held such diametrically opposed guidelines of what's supposed to make us happy. Using our example of money again, the Bible tells us that it is easier for a camel to pass through the eye of a needle than for a rich man to gain heaven. John Calvin, on the other hand, managed to convince a lot of people that God favors a rich man and is therefore heaven bound. So let us take a closer look at money, its incessant pursuit and what has just as often been denigrated as *filthy lucre*.

## Greedy or Lazy

| Why we will be unhappy with money | Why we will be unhappy without money | Why we will be bad in either case | Neutralizing argument |
|---|---|---|---|
| Dulls the spirit of enterprise. | It is want that crushes initiative, and demoralizes. | Unambitious, lazy | Money can just as easily induce a rich person to want to become richer as the lack of it can lead a poor person to pursue wealth. In any case, it would be presumptuous to claim that an ambitious person is likelier to be happy than one who is not. |
| Destroys independence and exposes us to the tides of fortune. | Money provides financial independence, and a poor person is more subject to the unforeseen. | Dependent, unresourceful | A rich person who is afraid of losing his money is as dependent on his having money as a poor person who is afraid of never having any. |
| Turns people's minds from higher intellectual and aesthetic endeavors. | Grinding poverty and lack of leisure discourage intellectual and aesthetic pursuits. | Materialistic, philistine, anti-intellectual | It is the rich who become patrons of the arts. Great cultural flowerings like Periclean Greece and the Renaissance were only possible with affluence. On the other hand, even the most dire circumstances cannot prevent artistic pursuits. Witness the Paleolithic cave paintings at Lascaux and Altamira. |

| | | | |
|---|---|---|---|
| Undermines honor, courage, and patriotism. | It is the disenfranchisement of the have-nots that distance people from accepted cultural standards. | Dishonorable, cowardly, unpatriotic | Honor and courage have never been the monopoly of any one economic class. Patriots have been recruited from those with large economic vested interests in their countries as well as the poor. If that were not the case, mercenaries notwithstanding, most armies would not have been raised, nor wars fought. |
| Weakens friendship, sympathy, and cooperation. | Financial uncertainty and fear for one's won survival undermines concern for others. | Cold, callous | Real friendship is, by definition, not changed by the vicissitudes of one's net worth. And while it is true that shared deprivation may engender sympathy and cooperation, so may mutual profit. |
| Spoils simple pleasures and a life that is close to nature. | Frees people from the drudgery of making a living and makes it more possible to enjoy. | Jaded, alienated from nature | Having money or not can't spoil the simple pleasures, nor can it alienate anyone from nature. All alienation is self-alienation—the belief that we will be led to make choices not in our best interests. |
| Lures people from God. | A rich person is more grateful to a bountiful God. | Ungrateful, arrogant | Gratitude is a state of mind available to anyone who chooses it. Arrogance is what is left over when we don't make that choice. |

| Engenders greed, war, and plunder. | Greed and envy are the products of deprivation and the knowledge that others have more. | Avaricious, envious | The have-nots are just as prone to greed as the haves. At least as many wars have been provoked by appealing to the have-nots as those motivated by the greed of the haves. |
| --- | --- | --- | --- |

What ought to be concluded from reviewing this table is that money is not the root of all evil. Wanting money or not wanting it, having it or not having it does not cause unhappiness. How we see ourselves in relation to money does that. When we want things while coming from that ego-defective perspective, the spectrum of our supposed failings vis-à-vis money can be broken down into two defects: we are either greedy or lazy. Greed is an evil of commission and laziness is an evil of omission. Between these extremes, exist all the possible ways in which we are said to be bad.

If laziness appears to describe a lack of desire, that is due to a failure to appreciate the difference between observing a behavior and judging it. Usually name-calling—laziness, in this case—is assigned to us by other people in order to get us to do what they want us to do. Frequently, name-callers are less interested in changing the behavior of the other than they are in maintaining their own. They often believe that by not condemning laziness in others, they might be tacitly endorsing what they have determined would be a bad tendency in themselves. In point of fact, only the dead are without desire, which makes laziness, as an explanation of human behavior, fictitious. Even the most passive person wants something. He or she may simply want to be left alone, to engage in any number of introspective activities, such as imagining, contemplating, remembering, planning, and fantasizing.

Acts of commission, on the other hand, appear to deserve different treatment from those of omission. Or do they? Presumably, greed is bad because the pursuit of money is motivated by excessive desire. *Excessive* often implies quantification but not in this instance. Any suggestion that wanting a million dollars would be greedy and wanting a lesser amount would not be is an arbitrary judgment. In this context, a moral judgment. A greedy person is not only one who wants as much money as can be accumulated, but also someone who is indifferent to the welfare of others. Greed implies that others are made to suffer for one's abundance. In effect, we have returned to the absence of a motive to explain a motive. What is now characterized as the indifference to the economic welfare of others sounds like a motive we have already discredited—laziness, albeit a sort of moral laziness. Nevertheless, it is a myth.

The so-called greedy person is not motivated by indifference, but rather by desire for wealth. So it doesn't even follow that wanting a lot of money for oneself necessarily works against the economic welfare of others. The "invisible hand" described by the eighteenth century economist Adam Smith benefits other people regardless of the self-centered interests of the person who creates wealth. Furthermore, suppose the so-called greedy person were juxtaposed to those who saw money as irrelevant to their welfare, would such a person still be considered greedy? The religious who take vows of poverty and others who are uninterested in money would not be affected by the greed of others. St. Francis, the paragon of saintliness, knew this better than anyone. The happiest of ascetics, he plunged into "blessed poverty" with the same passion that others pursue riches.

Standards of economic well being are determined by one's own belief about money and not someone else's self-serving desire. If no one else's welfare need be affected, then in what sense is a person bad for wanting what he or she wants? With the possible exception of a competitor's loss being the other game player's gain, which is the object of zero-sum games, no one takes pleasure in anyone's economic misfortune, unless he were feeling bad about himself at the outset. Oscar Wilde is supposed to have said, "It is not enough that I succeed; my friends must also fail." One wonders whether Wilde understood that *schadenfreude*—taking pleasure from another's misfortune—is only a kind of relief that someone else is not better than we are. The pursuit of money, if divorced from having something to prove, can never be motivated by greed. Even those who endorse the "greed is good" ideology don't understand this, suspicious as they are that they are not good and thus forced to engage in a form of doublethink, which will ultimately fail to give them what they really want—a clear conscience. When the ego has been removed from the idea of making money, the unsavory aura that often surrounds it disappears; its pursuit will then be driven by why it was invented in the first place—as a medium of exchange whose purpose was to buy goods and services, not self-esteem.

The conclusions are inescapable. If we are not bad for wanting what we want (greedy, selfish), not bad for getting what we want (aggressive, privileged), not bad for not wanting what we are supposed to want (lazy, apathetic, unambitious), we will most certainly not be bad for not getting what we do want (incompetent, stupid, indifferent). In a word, feeling bad is not the result of a discrepancy between what we want and the awareness that we might not get it. It is the belief that in failing to get what we want, we believe that something is wrong with us. Not getting what we want makes an unhappy person unhappy. It makes a happy person only inconvenienced. All of which returns us to the issue of low self-esteem, the true source of our unhappiness.

# 4

# The Myth Of The Gut Reaction–
# The Proactive Mind

*If you are distressed by anything external, the pain is not due
to the thing itself but to your estimate of it, and this you have
the power to revoke.*

*Marcus Aurelius*

*If we are to use this concept in a strictly scientific manner, it
is important to keep in mind that stress is an abstraction; it
has no independent existence.*

*Hans Selye*

In chapter two, we learned that self-deprecation is the source of unhappiness
and that any attempt at self-improvement can't work because of the
paradoxical and insoluble nature of negative self-reference. In chapter
three, we learned that it was not unsatisfied desires but self-deprecation,
again, that is at the heart of our unhappiness.

This chapter looks at still another account of human unhappiness:
the belief that feelings trump thinking. This way of thinking actually
assumes a split between the head and the heart, the mind and the body,
and suggests that emotions have a separate reality. It is a point of view that
changes the rules of communication, claiming that something as complex
and unfathomable as human emotion defies explanation, comparing it
to the way a mystical experience cannot be translated into language.
For the mystic, this hardly matters; the experience of bliss remains

intact despite any inability to express it. But those who are unhappy and adamantly hold to feelings as being separate from what we do in our head are hopelessly bogged down in inexpressible ignorance. Not being able to identify the source or the substance of your feelings, much less being unable to communicate them, makes any rational solution for unhappiness impossible.

This point of view leads people to believe that unhappiness is something we are fated to go through, that we can't know happiness unless we have known unhappiness. Although this makes no more sense than never enjoying sight unless we have been blind or good health unless we have been at death's door. Some investigators have even concluded that negative states are ennobling in some way, pointing out that spiritual revelation has often been preceded by a "dark night of the soul." Depressives have been known to say, "I had bottomed out and there was nowhere to go but up." The psychiatrist R. D. Laing believed madness to be an act of courage in an insane world. Still others can be persuasive in suggesting that negative emotions have an intelligence that aids us in engaging the world. They claim that certain negative emotions are basically adaptive and healthy which, to my mind, is only a secular variation of saying that suffering is good for the soul, but without the benefits of getting into heaven. Would any physician succeed in convincing his patient that a little bit of sickness might be good for his or her health? It seems to me that these theories are trying to convert mud into chocolate, meaning that if we don't know how to get rid of something, find a good use for it.

While these are well-intentioned efforts to justify the existence of negative states of mind, they are, at best, heroic measures whose ultimate aim is to make us feel better about feeling bad, simply more ways to help us cope. The interesting question is why should we only feel *better* and not *good?* In a nutshell, it's because better is perceived as good, but good is not perceived as better. However, feeling better but not good is only a palliative and settles for less than it should. Providing good reasons for feeling bad will not do, in my opinion, and so, for very practical reasons, we must demystify what we call "bad feelings."

All therapists recognize that feelings are modifiable. No school of psychotherapy could survive if it did not accept the notion that a change in self-awareness must have some effect on feelings. Theoretically, there are no limits as to how human beings might view themselves. If seeing things differently can make any difference, then, in principle, it can make every difference. Despite this, even the most optimistic therapies proceed on the basis that some unwanted feelings are unpreventable. In other words, there are permanent limits to how good we can feel. By whatever theoretical route, unhappiness seems to be locked into the human condition. Do any negative feelings, in fact, arise inside our bodies independently of what is going on in our heads? The fact that most people regard feelings as having a separate reality has important implications for happiness. Consider the statements:

*Jealousy* is my gut reaction to seeing her with him.

*Disgust* happens when I can't stomach something.

Whenever I hyperventilate, that tells me I'm *anxious.*

I get this sinking feeling of *despair.*

I have always suffered from *nervous* butterflies.

Is there an internal source of emotionality whose origin might be found in some part of our bodies other than our brains? Let's look at the case of Jennifer, a jealous wife.

## Jealousy

Setting: Jennifer is an attractive twenty-three-year old woman. She has been married for two years. She admits that her husband is a decent man, yet she complains of always being worried and finds herself compulsively calling her husband at work and trying to ferret out information such as whom he went to lunch with and what he might be "up to." When he comes home, she continues her interrogation. She recognizes the strain she is putting on the relationship; they argue constantly. She resolves to change but always fails. She is obsessed with the possibility of his being attracted to other women, and in spite of no real evidence, she suspects that he has been unfaithful. Recently they attended a party during which she went into a rage because he had spoken to a female guest. It was this incident that sparked her husband to insist that she seek help.

PS:         How can I help you?

Jennifer:   My jealousy is destroying my marriage.

PS:         How do you know that you are jealous?

Jennifer: Anytime I even think that my husband might be attracted to some other woman, I get this awful feeling, a sort of gut reaction, a knot in my stomach that never seems to leave me. I want you to help me to stop feeling this way.

PS: Do you think jealousy starts as a feeling or a thought process?

Jennifer: It seems to be more like a feeling.

PS: Do you think that what you are feeling in your body tells you what's going on in your head or the other way around?

Jennifer: I think it starts as a feeling. It's emotional.

PS: But you said that it happens when you think of the other woman.

Jennifer: Yes, but the feeling is there even when I'm not thinking about another woman.

PS: Let's say it's a package deal. One cannot exist without the other. If we eliminate one, we eliminate both. Since feelings seem to be more of a mystery than what we do in our head, let's start with what we know for certain is in your head, your suspicion that your husband might be attracted to other women.

Jennifer: Yes, that is my constant suspicion, and I can't seem to shake it.

PS: Let's find out why. What are you afraid it would mean if you stopped being suspicious?

Jennifer: If he knew that I trusted him and wasn't on top of him, I think that he would be more likely to stray.

PS: But there is something of a contradiction here. You started our conversation with the complaint that your jealous feelings were destroying your marriage, and now you seem to be saying that your suspicion, engendered by jealousy, will save your marriage by preventing him from straying.

| | |
|---|---|
| Jennifer: | I see the contradiction. It seems that I'm damned if I do and damned if I don't, but even knowing that is not going to change my feelings. |
| PS: | That's because we haven't identified the core contradiction yet. |
| Jennifer: | I don't understand. What is the core contradiction? |
| PS: | Your belief that you are inadequate. The way we can know that is by getting you in touch with the fact that your suspicion of the other women and your husband's possible interest in them is misplaced. Any such possible attraction only triggers what you already suspected might be wrong with you. |
| Jennifer: | I'm not clear about that connection. |
| PS: | It is important to understand that the only way that anyone can become jealous is by comparing themselves to a prospective rival and deciding that the other person is superior—sexier, prettier, smarter, and generally more desirable than they are. It should be clear to you that you couldn't be jealous of someone you believe to be your inferior. Why do you believe that you are inadequate? |
| Jennifer: | Are you asking what caused me to believe that I am inadequate? It probably started as a little girl? |
| PS: | That would be a when question. I'm asking why. |
| Jennifer: | I'm not sure I know what you mean. Don't you want to know how it all started? |
| PS: | I'm perfectly willing to listen if you want to tell me. But whatever your reasons were then, what are your reasons for believing it now? Were your parents unloving? |
| Jennifer: | No, but I still seemed to have been taught it. |
| PS: | But why did you learn it? Do you learn everything you are taught? |
| Jennifer: | No. |
| PS: | Then you must have learned it for some reason of your own. Why do you need to believe that you may not be good enough to be loved? |

| | |
|---|---|
| Jennifer: | I'm not sure. |
| PS: | What are you afraid it would mean if you assumed that you were worth loving? |
| Jennifer: | I always felt that if I presented myself that way, I would be seen as full of myself, and then no one would love me. |
| PS: | That was the starting contradiction. |
| Jennifer: | How can you be sure of that? |
| PS: | When anyone says they want to be loved, they can only want that to prove that they are worth loving. It is that core contradiction that set the stage for your jealousy and prefigured your whole world of irreconcilable contradictions. |
| Jennifer: | I don't see how wanting to be loved is a contradiction. |
| PS: | To begin with, you inadvertently made yourself needy, and the very thing you thought would make you more desirable made you less so; you became jealous. To make matters worse, even if you got the love that you wanted, you created a deficiency state, which means that you would have to continue to believe that you were unlovable to continue to get it. And finally, all these maneuvers rested on the most self-defeating contradiction of all, the belief that you had the power to prevent anyone from loving you. |
| Jennifer: | But you *can* make someone not love you. We both agree that my jealousy has affected my relationship with my husband. |
| PS: | Yes, but it is still up to him to decide to reject you, and he hasn't. Why did he urge you to talk to me if that weren't true? |
| Jennifer: | But I can't guarantee that he won't reject me. That is my greatest fear. |
| PS: | It is not rejection that you fear; he is only a mirror. You have been wasting your time thinking about what he believes about you, because you didn't understand that the final decision to love always rests with the lover and |

not the beloved. It is as impossible to prevent someone from loving you, as it is to make someone love you. If I still haven't made my point, you might consider that there are people who to this day love Hitler and Stalin. If two of the greatest mass murderers in the history of the world can't be prevented from being loved, it would be absurd to believe that you can.

Jennifer:     I still feel that everyone needs to be loved. Otherwise, what would the point of even having a relationship?

PS:     It is for the only reason that matters. Once you know that you cannot prevent anyone from loving you, it frees you to do what you were really born to do—to love, which is more enjoyable anyway. If you can get your husband to know what you know, you will get it back, not because you need it, but because you are giving him an opportunity to do what he was also born to do.

Jennifer:     Can I really trust that if didn't believe that I could prevent my husband from loving me, my feelings of jealousy would disappear?

PS:     Absolutely, jealousy is literally a paradox, the impossible result of trying to reconcile beliefs that are forever at odds with each other, namely that *needing* love, even when received, will ever produce feelings of *being* loved. The best you can get is relief. Do you understand the contradiction?

Jennifer:     I'm beginning to.

PS:     Has that knot in your stomach started to become untied?

Jennifer:     I see what you mean.

Jennifer is clearly someone who traces her troubles to her "stomach being in knots"—the so-called gut reaction. Most people regard this body-mind connection in a similar way. Jealousy is one example of this kind of thinking about emotions, but might not all negative emotions tend to be misunderstood this way? We know that truly discrete emotions do not exist. A flushed face, like a knotted stomach, could also be understood as a bodily response and not a thought process. Darwin observed that only human beings are capable of embarrassment. I believe this to be so because a blushing human being is a member of the only species that has the ability to find fault when they observe themselves. Dog lovers might dispute this. And although it must be conceded that dogs fall into a special category because of their long association with people and they often exhibit emotional responses that might resemble that of humans, unless it can be shown that they are able to disesteem themselves, we must be careful not to anthropomorphize–their "emotional" life must be of a different order. A chimpanzee, a primate whose DNA most closely resembles ours, conceivably might be able to recognize himself in a mirror, but he is incapable of calling himself ugly when he does. That is why he can't be unhappy.

Now consider the case of Emily as another example of how a physical expression of an emotion is mistakenly believed to precede what we do in our head.

## Embarrassment

Setting: Emily is thirty and looks twenty. She is a successful investment broker whose complaint is that she is easily embarrassed. Lately, it has gotten worse. She resents the fact that people tend to take a protective attitude toward her.

| | |
|---|---|
| Emily: | My problem seems to be that I blush at the slightest provocation, and it's been like that all my life. If I could just stop blushing, I could stop being embarrassed. |
| PS: | Could you be embarrassed if your face didn't turn red? |
| Emily: | No. That's how I know I'm embarrassed. |
| PS: | Do you think that if I could show you how not to blush, that would end your embarrassment? |
| Emily: | I think so. Since my face is always flushed when I become embarrassed, yes. |
| PS: | What do you think comes first, being embarrassed or your red face? |
| Emily: | They are the same thing. I can't separate them. But if I could at least stop my blushing, I would be less embarrassed, because they wouldn't know I was embarrassed. [Pause] I am starting to feel my face turning red now. |

PS:    Why is that?

Emily:    Because I am afraid that you think I'm some kind of immature little ninny.

PS:    Is that the problem? Or is it that you suspect that about yourself, regardless of what I think?

Emily:    I guess that's what I'd have to be doing. But I have come to that suspicion because of the way people treat me.

PS:    What do you mean?

Emily:    Like I'm some dear innocent child. Granted, parents are worrywarts, but I thought when I got my own place they'd respect my independence. But my mother goes on about a young girl living alone, as if I'm doing some daring, reckless thing. She calls me to ask if I acknowledged the birthday present from Aunt Marge. If a guy is around, forget it. I can't lift a finger. If I'm wheeling my bicycle onto the elevator, some man neighbor has to take it over. Even if I'm wrestling a bunch of junk mail out of my letterbox, it's "Here, let me do that." It's so dumb, and it makes me feel dumb.

PS:    Do you think other attractive young women have this problem?

Emily:    I was asking a girlfriend. She thought I was bragging. She implied that I was grousing because I hadn't found Mr. Right. Now, that truly is not my major concern at this point. My work is exciting. In terms of my goal setting, I'm ahead of the game. I want to get some travel in. Always being patronized spoils what I've achieved.

PS:    Are you sure you're being patronized? Professionally, at least, I don't think you would have come as far as you have if you didn't project some sense of authority. It sounds to me that you might be making yourself feel patronized.

Emily:    In the business arena, it is probably less true. Still, even here I get some guy needing to feel chivalrous. I was giving a ride to a broker I deal with, and when I went to unlock my car, he takes my car keys and says, "I'll get that." I could go on, but it never seems to stop.

PS: Do you do anything that induces people to treat you that way?

Emily: I think my looks have a lot to do with it.

PS: What is there about your appearance that leads you to believe that?

Emily: What ad nauseam has been referred to as my childlike innocence.

PS: You do have that look about you. I noticed that as I said that, you started to act girlish.

Emily: Yes. I always seem to do that when people look at me the way you just did.

PS: How did I look at you?

Emily: I can't quite put it into words.

PS: Might I propose "appreciatively?" You are nice to look at.

Emily: You're embarrassing me. Are you doing that deliberately?

PS: In a way, yes, but I think you would have to take responsibility for your embarrassment.

Emily: But I think you were flirting with me.

PS: My intention was purely professional. But even if it weren't, I still need your cooperation for you to become embarrassed.

Emily: Yes, that's true.

PS: Why do you embarrass yourself when someone looks at you appreciatively?

Emily: I guess I need to.

PS: And if you didn't, what do you think I would think?

Emily: That I was vain, conceited.

PS: That was pretty easy. You become embarrassed because you think I would judge you as conceited. Let's conduct an experiment. I'm going to say some things that are absolutely true, and as I'm saying them, I want you to keep the following question in mind: *If I accept what he says graciously and comfortably, will I be vain and conceited?*

Emily:     Okay.

PS:     When you walked into my office, I perceived a prepossessing, lovely, and sensual young woman. I saw a lithe body whose movements were balletic, and also that you had a sparkle and vivacity that was engaging in the extreme. I mean every word I say. How do you feel?

Emily:     Pretty comfortable at the outset, but then I started to get embarrassed.

PS:     Why?

Emily:     I started to suspect that maybe you were being insincere and simply using me as a guinea pig.

PS:     That may have crossed your mind, but I think you knew that I was perfectly sincere.

Emily:     How do you know that?

PS:     Because a lot of men have responded to you in that way. And the very fact that you fear being conceited already indicates that you are pretty well aware that you are as attractive as they say you are.

Emily:     Yes, that's so.

PS:     Emily, would you be conceited and vain if you graciously received compliments?

Emily:     I understand what you are saying, but how do I get people to stop being so damn protective … and sort of patting me on the head?

PS:     Ultimately, you have no final control over their behavior. But you will find that their behavior towards you will automatically change when they notice that you no longer become embarrassed. There would be no reason to protect what is no longer seen as fragile.

Emily:     There is one more thing that seems to embarrass me, and I don't think it has anything to do with my fear of appearing conceited.

PS:          What is that?

Emily:      It has to do with sexual matters. Not all the men that I come across are appreciative in a way that makes me act girlishly. For example, sometimes men smirk and even leer at me and make sexual comments, and it's so gross I could go through the floor. People say "just put him in his place," but I'm too embarrassed. I also cannot hear a raunchy joke without my face burning. Why do I feel so terribly embarrassed at those times?

PS:          Let's find out. Using the same question: *What are you afraid it would mean if you didn't turn red when sexual comments are made?*

Emily:      If I didn't, then they would think I'm like they are.

PS:          You turn red because that's your way of telling them you're not like them. Would you have to do that to yourself to know that you are not?

Emily:      I'm not sure.

PS:          You can be by simply reminding yourself that values do not simply disappear if you don't want them to. You are an attractive woman who knows who she is and what her values are. Embarrassment need play absolutely no part in your staying that way.

Emily:      That sounds good.

PS:          More important, it feels good. And maybe you have noticed you are not blushing—because you really do see that it is unnecessary.

Emily:      Yes, it does. I dearly hope I can hold on to it.

PS:          Trust that you can be trusted. In any case, we can always have another conversation as a reminder.

The clearest statement of how emotions might start in the gut, or viscera, was formulated by William James in what has come to be known as the James-Lange theory of emotions. He put it this way: "The bodily changes follow directly the perception of the exciting fact, and that our feelings of the same changes as they occur is the emotion." The key feature of this viewpoint is that the belief that when we experience an emotion, the bodily feelings comes first, ahead of what happens in our head.

## The Body and Emotions

As in all theories of emotions, we must account for the sequential relationship of at least three elements: what happens "out there,"—the environment and what is going on in our heads and in our bodies. We can diagram the visceral model as follows:

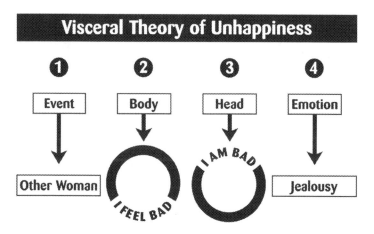

Notice that two elements in this schema are represented as circles, as they will be in all the subsequent diagrams in the book. The reason for this geometric highlighting is, as I hope to show, that what we do in our head and what happens in our body are the only relevant items worth considering regarding negative emotions. The underscoring also serves as a quick guide in fixing their relative positions in other theories of emotion. For instructional purposes, the same emotion—jealousy—will be used in all examples. Like most theories of emotion, the external event appears first in the sequence. *Unlike* most theories, the significant feature here is that the bodily response immediately follows the perception of the external event. We first feel bad and then become aware of it. The error that William James and some others who study emotions make is that they begin their analysis of negative emotions with "the perception of the exciting fact." The phrase is easily interchangeable with what is now simply termed the *event, stimulus, cause, object,* or more often, *stressor.* Whatever we call it, the common error is the belief that external phenomena are "intrinsically exciting."

It is not the perception of the "exciting fact" that leads to an emotional response; it is the negative perception of an external fact that makes it exciting, which, in effect, is the emotional response. It is only when we perceive an event negatively that we feel negatively, only when we label a thing as bad that we feel bad. Yet, while it is true that all negative emotional responses are necessarily produced by a negative evaluation, it does not follow that all negative evaluations necessarily produce an emotional response. It is only when these judgments and evaluations are perceived through a filter of self-deprecation, when one identifies in some way with the negative evaluation of the external event that we experience a negative emotion. A car that breaks down frequently is also psychologically bad when the negative evaluation of the car includes blaming oneself for having bought a lemon; a bad business deal has emotional implications only when the failed business venture is seen as evidence of personal ineptitude; a rejected romantic overture only hurts when we fault ourselves for being insufficiently attractive.

The same personalizing process occurs whether we negatively evaluate other people or feel negatively evaluated by them. It always lies within our power to reject condemnation, because it is always internally imposed even when it seems to be coming from the outside. Someone may indeed call you a bumbling idiot or a moral leper, but unless you suspect that they might be right, no unhappiness will result. It goes both ways; condemnation of others can be similarly internalized. "Moral outrage" and "righteous indignation" are the easiest examples of this process. They essentially describe the experience of feeling good about feeling bad: "I might be unhappy, but at least I have the consolation of being justified." However, that's not typically the kind of emotion that leads people to seek therapy. Feeling bad about feeling good does that.

In sum, negative evaluation of people and events produce negative emotions only when they are personalized. That happens in the following way: the percipient chooses what he perceives and so perforce he is in charge of his feelings but now, the choice having been made, it is still a matter of some practical importance as to how a visceral response figures into a full blown emotion. The notion that feelings that occur in our bodies might influence what is going on in our head is still an important issue because unless we understand its role in our emotional life, our understanding of unhappiness will remain incomplete.

Most people agree that what we feel in our body and what we do in our head are inseparable. Some believe that if we block or otherwise intervene on the bodily sensations of an emotion, it is possible to change it. The use of exercise, deep tissue massage, and hatha yoga take this point of view. While not arguing against the possible physical benefits of these prescriptions, I question whether they have anything to do with the prevention or elimination of negative emotions. When they "work," how do they work? Using these methods, do the bodily changes that might occur inform us in some way to prevent or eliminate negative emotions? What do they teach us about our so-called gut reaction?

The part of the nervous system that has the most to do with visceral responses is known as the *interoceptive process*. It receives internal stimulation from the alimentary tract, blood vessels, the bladder, and the glands and their ducts. As it happens, even in a normal, undisturbed state, this visceral system is quite insensitive. In a state of excitation, however, it is the individual's perception of these internal sensations that presumably helps him or her make discriminating contact with the world of inner feelings; they assume that internal sensation patterns give them an awareness that allows them to differentiate emotional states. In order to settle this question we might even ask an even more provocative one: *Are bodily feelings even necessary for an emotion to take place?*

Quadriplegics, who are the best people to answer this question, tell us that even though they are paralyzed from the neck down, they experience the whole range of emotions, commonly among which are despair and boredom. For those of us who have normal visceral feelings laboratory evidence has confirmed that bodily feelings are not very informative. What physiologists have found out about these excited states confirms this.

This general condition of excitation is known both technically and commonly as "stress." Its most famous researcher was Hans Selye. As a young medical student, Selye was struck by the fact that patients, regardless of their specific diseases, had a look of sameness about them. At that time, he referred to this condition as the "syndrome of being sick." It was not until years later that he had the opportunity to confirm his theory in the laboratory. He called his discovery the "General Adaptation Syndrome." He says: "It is difficult to see how such essentially different things as cold, heat, drugs, hormones, sorrow, and joy could provoke identical biochemical reactions in the body. Nevertheless this is the case; it can be demonstrated by highly objective, quantitative biochemical determinations that certain reactions are common to all types of exposure; it is immaterial whether the agent or situation we face is pleasant or unpleasant, all that counts is the intensity of the demand for readjustment and adaptation."

In other words, from the point of view of what observably and measurably takes place in our bodies, it does not matter whether a person is undergoing an infection, experiencing an orgasm or a dentist's drill, the stress reaction is biochemically the same. I do not mean to say that there may not be certain specific reactions in addition to the generalized state of arousal when the stress is physiologically induced, such as the direct result of a trauma-producing agent. Specific, observable bodily reactions will also occur. Malaria produces fever; extreme cold causes shivering; injury leads to inflammation. These different stimuli call up very different physical, symptomatic expressions. This is not the case when stress is psychologically induced.

Cross-cultural researchers have even tried to connect facial expressions to specific emotions, which suggest the possibility that emotions might originate in some other region of our body. The first complication with physiognomy is that despite the observation that cross-cultural studies seem to indicate that some emotions may have specific facial expressions, it has also been observed that these same facial expressions can be easily misunderstood. Photographs cropped of their social settings can produce surprising misinterpretations. In one photograph, an expression that appeared agonized turns out, when put back in context, to be the exhilaration of a lottery winner. In another, an expression of seeming joy is the contorted grimace of a man pinned under collapsed masonry.

Some of us have had real life experiences that would underscore the chameleon nature of emotional expression. When we get bad news, we may cry, gasp, and shake, but we may do the same when overcome with joy. Even laughter can be the result of the comical or delirium. Nevertheless, mimicry and related approaches in the teaching of acting hold the view that by reconstructing facial configurations that are allegedly correlated to a specific emotion, the actor will be able to experience the full-blown emotion. But even if successful, facial movements, like any observable behavior associated with an emotion, is never where the negative emotions originate. Bad feelings, then, still begin with self-deprecation, and its origin can only take place in our heads. That is why the physiognomy of specific emotions is of incidental significance.

In sum, bodily feelings and expressions are either a response to external and internal agents that materially impinge directly on our bodies, or they are the result of what is going on in our heads, but in every case, the visceral arousal is nonspecific. Beyond informing us of "the intensity of the demand for readjustment and adaptation," as Selye described, internal bodily agitations tell us nothing. It is clear that the psychological meaning of gut reactions is determined by what we believe; bodily feelings do not have a logic of their own. They take on meaning only when we believe something before we get them and, sometimes, after we get them. But in the latter instance, only when those feelings have a strictly physical cause, as in an illness or the ingestion of a drug that may mimic an emotion, and are sometimes misinterpreted as such. (Adrenaline can produce such a misinterpretation, which I will show in the next chapter). Otherwise, bad feelings always *follow* awareness, never the other way around. That is why getting in touch with one's feelings misses the point. The real solution to our problem of feeling bad is not to get in touch with our feelings, but to get in touch with our beliefs.

# 5

# Biochemistry–Never A Love Potion

*Serotonin–enhancing antidepressants(such as Prozac and many others)can jeopardize feelings of romantic love, feelings of attachment to a spouse or partner.*

*Helen Fisher*

We hear a lot nowadays about biochemical imbalance and its possible link to negative emotional states. The question is: can such substances, called neurotransmitters, affect the brain in such a way so as to make us unhappy? Is the origin of depression, for example, simply a question of understanding how these chemical substances work in nerve cells? Although there are hundreds of these neurotransmitters, serotonin seems to have gained the most interest in recent years. Serotonin, or rather the lack of it, has been implicated in depression. Prozac and a group of closely related drugs such as Paxil, Effexor, Celexa, Lexapro, and Zoloft belong to a whole new generation of anti-depressants known as SSRIs—selective serotonin reuptake inhibitors.

Serotonin is made in the nerve cell, or *neuron*, and then released from the nerve ending into a small space known as the synapse, which lies between two nerve endings. It acts as a chemical messenger between the nerves. Normally, serotonin stays there for a short time, is used up, degraded, and returned to the neuron that produced it for further use. That return is called *reuptake*. SSRIs inhibit the reuptake process; the theory being that by blocking the reuptake and thus keeping the serotonin in the synapse longer, the increase of serotonin in the synapse will alleviate the emotional disorder. Although originally designed to treat depression and, later, obsessive-compulsive disorders, SSRIs are now being prescribed for eating disorders, phobias, shyness, anxiety, panic attacks, alcohol addiction, emotional problems in children and adolescents, chronic fatigue syndrome, migraine headaches, and premenstrual syndrome (PMS). They have even been prescribed for normal people as "personality enhancers." Following this line of thinking, it would appear that psychopharmacologists are coming close to claiming that the "soma" that produced contentment in Aldous Huxley's novel *Brave New World* is not a fanciful quest.

Of late, however, Prozac and its psychotropic cousins have had their efficacy claims come under attack, and it may be due to the very theory of "biochemical imbalance" itself. Imbalance implies that there is too much or too little of something, which in this case are brain chemicals. What *are* brain chemicals, and can they be measured? Usually, when dealing with physical disorders, biochemical imbalances can be determined with precision. Doctors know the effects of too much or too little insulin, glucose, this or that vitamin deficiency, and hormonal imbalances of various kinds. Grave's disease (hyperthyroidism) and Cushing's syndrome (adrenocortical hormone excess) are two examples of how such imbalances affect the body. The theory of chemical imbalance and its effects on mental states, however, is not as secure; much less is known about the brain than other organs of the body. How neurotransmitters really work and how they are interrelated is still a profound mystery. What we reliably know about serotonin is that its presence helps us modulate raw information and imparts emotional tone. In other words, while other neurotransmitters help us perceive the level of water in a glass, serotonin helps us decide whether it is half-full or half-empty. Despite this evidence, the final decision as to how we perceive things is decided by us.

To better understand how that happens, let's look at a common psychological complaint—PMS, whose origin is *said to be* caused by changes in a woman's body chemistry. The "raging hormone" theory has been around a lot longer than the newly acquired knowledge of neurotransmitters, but the general idea is the same, namely, that altered biochemistry causes depression. This point of view contains some troublesome implications. We know that depression always entails low self-esteem, which means biochemists who aim to treat PMS might be claiming that it is possible to synthesize a biochemical that will transform self-hate into self-love. Ironically, psychotropic medication appears to do the opposite. Seventy percent of people who take SSRIs complain that their ability to feel love has been compromised, making it harder to fall in love and to stay in love. Nevertheless, twenty-five hundred years have elapsed and the dream of discovering what the ancients called a love potion—a chemical compound aimed at transforming hate into love—still persists. The question that begs to be asked is, *can love*, whatever its object—self, God, family, spouse, nature, art, or country—*be achieved via a psychoactive drug?* The following dialogue might answer that question. It demonstrates that, while not disputing the physical reality of altered biochemistry, it is how a woman perceives herself that ultimately produces her depression.

## Depression

Setting: Diane is thirty-five years old. She is a systems analyst with an insurance company. She hopes to go into private consultancy; if she can build up a sufficient clientele. She has struggled with depression for most of her adult life.

| | |
|---|---|
| Diane: | I have terrible PMS. |
| PS: | What does that mean? |
| Diane: | Don't you know? |
| PS: | I'd rather hear what you mean by it. |
| Diane: | I have a hormonal imbalance. |
| PS: | Have you tried to balance your hormones? |
| Diane: | Yes. |
| PS: | With unsuccessful results, I gather. |
| Diane: | Not totally. |
| PS: | But not enough, apparently, or you wouldn't be here talking to me. You know I don't deal with drugs. |
| Dian: | Yes, I know. |
| PS: | And since all you and I will be doing is talking, I imagine you're not altogether sure that your depression is a chemical question. |
| Diane: | I would like to believe that just talking it out could eliminate my depression. |
| PS: | But you're doubtful. |

| | |
|---|---|
| Diane: | It just seems to feel that it is biochemical. I can feel something happening in my body when I get depressed. In fact, it often seems to happen in the night. I get the impression that you think I'm mistaken. |
| PS: | Not at all. I don't deny that what you are feeling is something biochemical. But is that the real question? |
| Diane: | Then what is? |
| PS: | The question is does your depression start biochemically? |
| Diane: | Sure it does. That is certainly true when I get my period. My god, when I am about to get my period, I'm impossible. It's been like that most of my adult life. After all, PMS is a recognized condition. Only I've got it really heavy duty. |
| PS: | The problem with the raging hormone theory is that it is somewhat confusing. At what point do you know you're depressed? |
| Diane: | I get bloated, cramps, lethargic, bitchy, weepy. I start to feel ugly. That is the standard reaction. Setting it up for everybody to think, "Oh, she's got the rag on," which annoys the hell out of me. |
| PS: | I would like to point something out. You start out by describing how you feel in your body. Then, almost imperceptibly, you go into what's going on in your head. "Bloated" and "cramps" refer to what you can observe going on in your body. "Lethargy" is more borderline. It can be used objectively to describe reduced energy caused by hormonal changes. If metabolic processes are depressed, the body is literally depressed. But here we come to a subtle transition. At this point, the loss of energy is associated with subjective meanings: you mention "bitchy," "weepy," and "ugly." |
| Diane: | It's like everything gets to me then. |
| PS: | Now, at what point does *bloated* and *crampy* lead to lethargic and then end up feeling bitchy, weepy, and ugly? At what point does physical lassitude turn into psychological depression? There's a leap here: from a fact |

|        |                                                                 |
|--------|-----------------------------------------------------------------|
|        | to a judgment of that fact. Besides, you have left out the main psychological element in depression. |
| Diane: | What's that? |
| PS:    | I think you know what that is. |
| Diane: | You mean that I feel bad about myself? |
| PS:    | Would you agree that it would be impossible to be depressed and not have low self-esteem? |
| Diane: | Sure, because then you know that you're at your very worst, full of self-pity. |
| PS:    | I am trying to pinpoint when metabolic changes in the body turns into psychological depression. According to *you*, the hormonal change in some way lowers your self-esteem. According to *me*, you are unconsciously using those changes to put yourself down. According to *you*, your feeling good depends on future advances in biochemical research. According to *me*, your psychological well-being depends on your understanding what you are doing to yourself right now. |
| Diane: | How do we find out which of us is right? |
| PS:    | Which of us would you like to be right? |
| Diane: | I would like to think that I could kick my depression without drugs. |
| PS:    | Do you think you could want that if you didn't think it was possible to begin with? |
| Diane: | Wanting it doesn't make it so. |
| PS:    | Don't be so sure. |
| Diane: | I'm starting to feel anxious. Why do I feel hesitant all of a sudden? |
| PS:    | For the unconscious reason I mentioned earlier. We'll deal with that in a minute. But unless you are convinced that your problem is psychological and not chemical, we'll never get there. Offhand, do you think it's possible for alcohol to produce self-esteem? |
| Diane: | Of course not. |

PS:     I was hoping you would think that. Why do you think people drink?

Diane:  For a lot of reasons.

PS:     Not really. They all drink to feel good. And in the short run, it usually achieves that objective. If it didn't, no one would do it. Of course, what they mean by feeling good is relief from feeling bad. And that's not the same as having self-esteem.

Diane:  That may be true of alcohol, but is it true of all drugs?

PS:     Do you believe that a drug will be created that will make people like themselves?

Diane:  When you put it that way, it seems unlikely. But in spite of what you say, it still seems to me that my period makes me feel bad about myself.

PS:     Perhaps if we looked at the experience a little more closely, we might find out what really happens to you. In addition to feeling bitchy, what other thoughts do you have?

Diane:  I just feel I'm at my worst, no good for anything, gross.

PS:     If you had undergone surgery, and were in the process of recuperating, you would also not be at your best. Would you feel gross then?

Diane:  No.

PS:     Then what is there about this physical indisposition that is any different? Why do you see yourself as repugnant in one case and not in the other?

Diane:  Well, at least after an operation, people would bring me flowers.

PS:     That might be a perk, but that wouldn't solve your problem. Do you know the biological function of menstruation?

Diane:  Among other things, it's a cleansing process.

PS:     Yes, a process that evolved over millennia and, as it turns out, crucial to your to your health and survival.

Diane:  That's not what I'm thinking at the time. That's certainly not part of my experience.

PS:      I know. It's significant that the core reason for your period has escaped you. I'm reminding you, because that awareness alone could change your experience.

Diane:      If only menstruation happened once a year instead of once a month.

PS:      Or that the cleansing process might be accomplished by blowing your nose or a quick burp or two. But there's no point with arguing with nature. That's the way it is. In any case, is there any reason you can't appreciate the fact that your body is functioning exactly the way it was meant to?

Diane:      Are you trying to get me to like it?

PS:      That might be a little ambitious at this stage. I'll settle for your not calling yourself gross. Why would you call this necessary biological process or the sensations that go with it ugly?

Diane:      I guess I'm saying the same thing, but I just feel so physically unattractive when I get my period. I feel so unsexy.

PS:      Of course, you could feel sexy even with what is going on in your body but if you decide otherwise, why aren't you allowed to feel unsexy?

Diane:      Because if I feel unsexy, then no one else will find me sexy either. And if I'm not sexy, I'm nothing.

PS:      Why do you believe you're nothing when you are not sexy?

Diane:      This may sound weird, but I think in some way it makes me more desirable.

PS:      How does calling yourself nothing make you more desirable?

Diane:      I don't know. It just seems to protect me in some way.

PS:      You're doing fine. Let's start with how you might be protecting yourself. What are you protecting yourself against?

Diane:      Against being judged unattractive.

PS:    How does your calling yourself unattractive do that?

Diane:    If I'm already feeling unattractive, I get the jump on other people. Then it won't feel as bad if someone else says it. I guess it's like protecting myself from a fall. It's better to fall from a two-story building than a skyscraper.

PS:    I once heard a window washer of skyscrapers being asked if he became more anxious when he was very high up. He said no, because he would be dead no matter where he fell from. Why do you think I tell you that?

Diane:    Meaning dead is dead.

PS:    Yes, and feeling bad is feeling bad. It's a superstition to believe that you protect yourself from possible disappointment by preparing for it.

Diane:    I think you're wrong there. If you remind yourself beforehand that things may not work out, it does help you to feel less disappointed.

S:    Yes, but not the way *you* do it. It is one thing to acknowledge that the future is always uncertain. It's something else to go into how bad you'll feel if things don't work out. You make yourself feel unattractive to shield yourself from the possibility that others may think that. So you're going around in a suit of armor. The very protection that you put on against people finding you unattractive is apt to produce the result you're afraid of. What could make you more unattractive than your fear that you are?

Diane:    I see what you're saying. Why do I still fight the idea of dropping it completely? Why do I still need to make myself feel unattractive?

PS:    That must have to do with what you said earlier. Remember, you said that unless you believed you were unattractive, you would never be attractive. What do you mean by that?

Diane:    If I never doubted my attractiveness, I mightn't do all the stuff that keeps me attractive.

PS:    Would either of those things really happen, if you stopped making yourself feel ugly? Think before you answer.

Diane:          (a very long pause) No.

Diane's belief that there is a chemically induced cause-and-effect chain that determines our feelings is something we all run into all the time:

I get *depressed* when I get my period.

Too much sugar makes me *moody*.

When he drinks, he gets *hostile*.

The lack of tryptophan causes sleeplessness and *anxiety*.

*Anger* is produced by too much testosterone.

Caffeine makes me *irritable*.

One of the most impressive psychological experiments in modern times aimed at unraveling the mystery of emotions was conducted by the psychologist Stanley Schachter. His experiment was designed to find out if altered biochemistry was the crucial factor in the production of an emotion. In Schachter's experiment, he misled a group of students into believing that he was testing a new drug. In reality, he gave one group adrenaline, a substance known to cause dramatic, "emotional" sensations such as a flushed skin and accelerated pulse. To another group he gave a tranquilizer. To the third, a control group, he gave a simple saline solution. He found that the group aroused by adrenaline was more elated in agreeable situations, more annoyed in irritating situations, and even more amused in comic situations than those students given the placebo. Not unexpectedly, the tranquilized group was the least responsive.

From this study, Schachter concluded that, despite the intensity of the response or the lack of it, it was not biochemistry but rather the social context that defined a specific emotion. What is really compelling is that as a psychologist investigating stressful responses, his results were remarkably similar to those conducted by the earlier mentioned Hans Selye, the physiologist who researched stressful states. In both cases, stress–the bodily feeling–is a stereotyped state of arousal to which good and bad qualities are attributed. Stress becomes *distress* either before or after it is worked over by something in our heads.

It should be mentioned that "attribution theory," as this is called, deals with all the same elements as the visceral model, with one important difference. In this sequence, self-observation immediately followed the external event, which, in turn, was followed by the bodily feeling. In short, people felt emotions in response to their social surroundings. Since Schachter defined the external event as a social situation, we will call this the *situational model.*

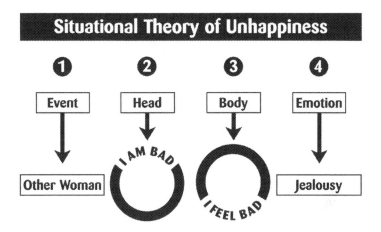

Schachter's experiment is significant because he redefined the external event in situational terms. He correctly recognized the significance of the social context in influencing our emotions. What is different, among other things, is the sequence of events. In this model, self-perception—what we do in our heads—precedes what we feel in our body. It is also important to mention that while attribution theory was a fresh direction in a world of conflicting research, and for many a final explanation of emotionality, Schachter's experimental results have not been readily duplicated. Some experimenters have even claimed that adrenaline administered to their subjects produced full-blown emotions, regardless of the social circumstances.

How are we to take all this? If the results of psychological experiments with human beings often seem inconclusive and contradictory, it is because the experimenters can never overcome one centrally important limitation. They can never be sure, at any given moment, how the human subject will choose to view him or herself, regardless of the situation. If self-deprecation can occur under any social or biochemical circumstances, then the results of conducting emotional experiments using human subjects will always be problematic.

Look at it this way: A social situation, by definition, provides its participants with a set of expectations of what is regarded as appropriate behavior. We are expected to feel happy at weddings and sad (or at least solemn) at funerals. Observably, most of the time the personal expectations of the participants in these social contexts are in agreement with the expectations defined by the social context. But that doesn't always happen. Wedding guests can also feel depressed or envious because they believe that they are not good enough for anyone to want to marry them. At a funeral where grief is expected, participants may also feel elated, lucky to be alive, or glad that the deceased is out of their lives. In the end, what determines a negative emotion is not the social context but a negative self-perception, which may or may not occur in a social setting with a clearly defined emotional protocol. This also explains why experimenters were able to produce results diametrically opposed to Schachter's and why subjects injected with adrenaline were also able to experience full-blown emotions. Just as negative self-perception may or may not be guided by a social context, it may or may not be guided by a biochemical change in one's body. The mistake in the logic of the biochemical explanation is in thinking that because a social situation was unnecessary to the production of an emotion, it was therefore induced by the adrenaline. In my view, it was not.

Adrenaline has a number of medical uses, one of which is its use in the treatment of asthma (usually as epinephrine). A number of years ago, I had an asthmatic reaction that required an injection of adrenaline, a chemical substance known to be an excellent bronchial dilator. But in this instance, the attending physician neglected to inform me of the side effects of the drug. Driving home, I started to experience palpitations, tremors, a racing pulse, and a flushed face. For a moment, I believed I was having a cardiovascular incident or an anxiety attack. Then I remembered that adrenaline had these "sympathomimetic" properties, which mimic the effects of the sympathetic nervous system.

What might have become a full-blown anxiety attack was instantly converted into what is known in the psychological literature as a "cold emotion." A cold emotion can be defined as an "as if" experience. It has all the physiological trappings of an emotion with none of its associated negative feelings. What this shows is that adrenaline, like all psychoactive drugs, can only excite or sedate nervous systems. They cannot force people to view themselves favorably or unfavorably; they cannot create good or bad self-perceptions.

That is why psychotropic drugs "work" only some of the time. If the object of taking drugs is to improve how one feels, the reason for the uncertain results is that the drug taker may feel differently about himself at different times. Moreover, it has always been true that all psychoactive drugs have different effects on different people. Why? Because people are different. Longitudinal studies of drug users have revealed that some lifetime, heroin users are able to use the drug sparingly for years without becoming addicted. When Quaaludes were misused and in fashion as aphrodisiacs, some people became amorous and others just got sleepy. I had a client for whom it was a point of pride not to cooperate when he was administered sodium pentothal. He delighted in lying when given the "truth serum." We also know that *good* trips and *bad* trips are not created by lysergic acid. LSD only makes hallucinations possible. The people who ingest it script their content. And it is a well-known phenomenon, especially to bartenders, that some people who drink what they believe to be alcohol will often feel "high" even where there's no alcohol consumed.

Recent research has revived interest in the placebo effect and it was discovered that its impact proved far greater than was formerly thought. It has been estimated that between 35 and 75 percent of patients benefit from taking chemically inactive pills. Sham knee operations for arthritis and inert substance-inhalers for asthmatics have been shown to be as helpful as conventional therapeutic measures. Keep in mind that these results are describing how the mind effectively handles medical conditions. It follows that psychological disorders would be even more placebo-sensitive. Numerous clinical trials have been conducted to determine the relevance of the placebo effect when taking antidepressants, and it appears that it is the *expectation of improvement,* not necessarily any changes in brain chemistry that account for a drug's effectiveness. The irresistible implication is that neither viscera nor biochemistry are the source of negative states. Bad feelings are always descriptive of an individual's response and never of the internal stimulus conditions. Drugs impinging on the nervous system may provide the music, but it is we who write the lyrics and we who choose the dance.

# 6

# Genes—None For Self-Esteem

*Temperamental phenomena cannot be reduced to biology.*
Jerome Kagan

*We will probably find genes that influence behavior. But I'm quite certain we won't find genes that* determine *behavior.*
Lynn Jorde

*Now imagine there's one hundred genes involved, interacting with each other and with the environment. I just think it's a non-starter to talk about genetic engineering.*
Robert Plomin

The popular 1956 horror movie *The Bad Seed* began as a bestselling novel, which turned into an acclaimed Broadway play, suggesting a compelling theme.[4] The theme proposes that some people might be born innately evil. In literature, as in society, that's hardly a new idea. The novelist John Steinbeck examines the same notion in *East of Eden*. In his description of the diabolical child, Cathy, he wrote that she even had feet "like little hooves." More recently, Oliver Stone theorized in his movie, *Natural Born Killers,* that malevolence may be hereditary. That personality characteristics that cause us to harm others might be inherited is a serious matter. It is the biological equivalent of original sin. Only worse. If evil were gene-driven,

---

4   The novel was written by William March, adapted for the stage by Maxwell Anderson, and then adapted again by John Lee Mahin into an Academy Award-nominated film directed by Mervyn Leroy.

it would make the theological doctrine of original sin pale. Original sin only claims that while human nature inclines toward evil, each of us can find salvation through faith and force of will. Bad seeds, on the other hand, are damned beyond redemption from the moment of their birth. Their evil ways would be as impossible to change as the color of their eyes.

While this may be an exciting theme for the theater and the movies, it's an idea that is completely unproven. Nevertheless, there continues to be a certain mystique that surrounds the idea of inborn or inherited psychological traits. The latest scientific incarnation of this point of view is *behavioral genetics*. At first glance, its point of view doesn't seem to deviate much from common sense. We single out the black sheep of a family and whisper, "He's no good; he never was any good." Further, the concept of genetic predisposition to certain things is sometimes expanded to include whole societies or nationalities. We may believe that those full-of-blarney Irish like to drink too much, or that the passionate Latins are good lovers with terrible tempers, or that the brooding Russian and Nordic peoples are more prone to depression.

Physiologists have made a fair case for natural-born baseball players, pilots, ballet dancers, and the like. On more secure biological grounds, geneticists have discovered a single-gene basis for diseases like Down syndrome, spinal bifida, Tay-Sachs, and cystic fibrosis. So, since there are indications that genes are linked to *certain* physical capacities, conditions, and disorders, the logical leap is that there might be similar genetic relationships to personal temperament, which is to say behavioral and psychological traits. It has long been suspected that *behaviors* such as schizophrenia, alcoholism, sexual preference, and even shyness are genetically based. For decades, we were led to believe that human beings could be classified as A or B personality types, that aggressive and non-aggressive behavior were genetically determined. Another theory that once had the imprint of scientific respectability concerned the extra Y chromosome, which allegedly predisposed men to be more violent. Thus far, the suspect gene(s) have not been identified and both theories have been generally discredited.

These developments call into question the whole program of psychological predispositions, specifically the claim that low self-esteem and unhappiness may be locked somewhere in our genes. Nevertheless, the proposal that negative emotions have genetic roots has a long and stubborn history, and so the errant *seed* is an idea that never seems to go out of fashion. Consider how often we make statements concerning inherited tendencies:

*Jealousy* is an adaptive reaction to territorial encroachment.

I have a high-strung and *nervous* temperament.

My father was also very *moody.*

*Depression* runs in her family.

He's a naturally *suspicious* type.

My mother's *panic attacks* started when she was just my age.

Despite its importance and potential, and despite the hyperbolic claims of a few geneticists, genetics still remains one of the most baffling fields of biological research. With all the advances in the study of human genetics, including our increased understanding of the biochemistry of single genes and the decoding of the genome, we remain completely ignorant of the ways in which genes interact with each other and with environmental factors to produce a unique human being. Researchers have only begun to study the impact of genes on human physical development. When it comes to the interaction of genes with the environment in a person's psychological development and emotional life, everything is pure speculation. Even under the best of laboratory conditions, working with non-human social animals, it is virtually impossible to know to what degree the behavior being observed is due to heredity or to the environment. Leaving aside the issue of the assumed continuity between animal and human behavior, even on the grossest statistical level, no real estimates of the relative importance of genetic and environmental factors on human physical development can be made.

For one thing, unlike genes that may be responsible for physical traits, the genes putatively responsible for personality traits such as hostility, anxiety, shyness, extraversion, and impulsiveness do not *cause* people to become that way. Presumably, they are chemicals that guide other chemicals. Behavioral genes are less like switches and more like subtle prods. But even if those anticipated *errant* genes were discovered, it would still be necessary to specify how they interacted with other genes and with the environment in order to produce a specific behavior. As to how either of these interactions might be explained, we know nothing. Moreover, it seems certain to remain that way. Biologists tell us that the task of disentangling the connection between a gene and the environment, even with simpler organisms, is an extraordinarily difficult enterprise.

In order to dramatize this point, let's look at an example of good genetic science for inherited physical characteristics and compare that with bad genetic science for inherited psychological characteristics. The Chinese primula or primrose is a garden flower that has a red strain and a white strain. When the two strains are crossed, they will produce the following variety of offspring: one pale red, two pink, and one white flower. When the red-flowered plant is grown in a hothouse at a temperature of ninety-five degrees or more over several generations, its flowers will become white and will remain white indefinitely—only at that temperature. If you return it to the garden, where the temperature falls below ninety-five degrees, it will become red again. On the molecular level, why this happens is still not understood, but the behavior is unerringly predictable. We know that the genetic predisposition exists, and we know the exact, quantifiable, environmental conditions that will cause the plant to behave the way it does. This sort of mathematically precise nature–nurture connection is relatively rare, even when trying to explain biological heritability. What are the chances of achieving that kind of precision in things psychological?

Consider a psychological experiment conducted by the Harvard psychologist Jerome Kagan. In his book *Galen's Prophecy,* Kagan describes an experiment in which he tried to determine a possible link between shyness and genetics. He found that some infants, when stimulated, showed symptoms of distress by crying and thrashing their limbs. Others remained unaffected or became relaxed with the same stimulation. Still others could not be categorized, because they exhibited different reactions of shyness or outgoingness. Using those behavioral criteria, he grouped them into shy, uninhibited, and uncategorizable. Follow-up experiments through the subjects' childhood and adolescence produced all manner of outcomes. About half of both the shy and the uninhibited children retained these traits during childhood and adolescence. Some shy infants later became outgoing, and some uninhibited infants became sullen and introverted in later years. Dr. Kagan concluded, "Temperamental phenomena cannot be reduced to biology." The problem with the experiment, like all psychological studies dealing with infants is what is really being observed. Withdrawal from strangers to a newborn is an entirely different behavior than the same observed behavior in an adult. "Shyness" in an infant has nothing to do with how they see themselves, but for an adult, it has everything to do with it.

Evolutionary psychology, the other incarnation of gene theory, takes another approach. Like the behavioral geneticists, these theorists seek to explain human behavior genetically, but in a different way. Whereas behavioral geneticists focus on genetic traits that make individuals different, evolutionary psychologists zero in on traits that human beings share. They also differ in that their evolutionary outlook makes for a strictly *retrodictive* science, hypothesizing about events that *might have occurred* in the past. It has no predictive power, because evolution cannot be tweaked. Still, they try to peer at human behavior through the filter of natural selection.

In 1975, in an attempt to answer some of the questions regarding the relationship between evolution and human psychology, Harvard biologist Edward O. Wilson developed a new field of study that he called "sociobiology." He tried to develop the foundation for a detailed theory of human nature in which all behavior is determined by heredity and evolution. Hoping to do justice to the complexity of social life, of which emotionality is an important part, he tried to show that human traits such as bellicosity, shyness, selfishness, and altruism stem from our primordial need to propagate our genes. All behavior, which includes one's social and emotional life, is to be seen as inherited and adaptive.

While we must concede that heredity and evolution provide us with powerful explanations for much of biological behavior, it doesn't follow that all behavior can be understood in those terms. *After all, we are trying to understand the most important issue that has ever occupied human consciousness, namely, consciousness itself and its relationship to happiness.* Will geneticists ever discover the gene for low self-esteem, determine how it interacts with other genes, and then proceed to discover the precise environmental conditions that will allow it to express itself? How might geneticists help people who are destroying their lives with jealousy, for example? Would they snip out the bad DNA that predisposes them to be jealous or possibly replace it with the good DNA. And failing that, will they be able to specify the environmental conditions that would suppress its emotional expression and ultimately allow self-esteem to flourish? Isn't jealousy, like all negative emotions, a mindset *and* a feeling? And if it is that, can it really be understood in terms of some discoverable DNA? Might not unhappiness be some emergent experience that is generated by a human being, which is allowed by heredity but not dominated by it? Isn't jealousy an emotion that is the result of what we believe about ourselves? If so, how can a belief really be inherited?

Consider the idea of natural selection as it might pertain to jealousy. Natural selection tells us that behavior, in general, ought to be viewed as *coping mechanisms* that are transmitted by the survivors of one generation for the survival of the next. An emotion like jealousy, it might be claimed, is part of our evolutionary history, a primitive remnant of a possibly still useful defense against territorial encroachment. A jealous woman has often been described as "fighting like a tigress for her man." When she is rejected, the implied message is that she is unsuitable for mating and unable to contribute to the survival of the species. It's the evolutionary explanation for "hell hath no fury like that of a woman scorned."

The problem with this survival account of jealousy is not hard to find. To begin with, not all women are jealous. Why should there be any differences? If emotions are indeed adaptive coping mechanisms, why don't all members of the species inherit the same self-protective responses? A species, after all, can only have evolved because it inherited identifiable characteristics that allowed its members to behave in ways that would ensure its survival. There are no short-necked giraffes, for example. Furthermore, if the jealousy gene existed as a mechanism of self-protection and was triggered when an environmental threat to the physical integrity of the family appeared, it would abate when the interloper departed. Human jealousy goes far beyond territoriality. It is a chronic self-deprecating emotional state that stays with a person with or without an immediate environmental threat. A person who is jealous suffers the most intensely persistent feelings of inadequacy, not the flash reaction of someone trying to protect her territory from encroachment. This is the young woman who might linger in the coatroom, re-combing her hair because she can't psych herself up to go out and join the party where her husband's old girlfriend is a guest. Most certainly, whatever it is that changes survival pressures cannot account for a seemingly reflexive response becoming a sustained emotional problem. Moreover, if the purpose of jealousy was designed to maintain family integrity, it does exactly the opposite. Ask any marriage counselor how many marriages have been destroyed because of suspicions engendered by jealousy and more often than not without any justification.

I believe there is a deeper explanatory principle at work here. This ought not be so startling since Darwin himself emphasized that non-adaptive changes also occur during evolution. Genetics and natural selection claim only to deal with inherited characteristics and their relationship to survival. Neither of these notions can account for any number of human traits, among which is the most uniquely important characteristic of the human species: our acquisition of language. Noam Chomsky, the towering figure in modern linguistics, has stated that the origin of language cannot be explained by appealing to evolution. There is no obvious reason why language should have appeared in the first place, and yet it is stunningly paradoxical that it is essentially through language that we are able to form a personal identity and, by extension, disesteem ourselves.

Among the other behaviors that natural selection fails to explain are deathbed confessions, laughter, grief, religious vows, saintliness, celibacy, abortion, infanticide, voluntary childlessness, homosexuality, and art. What does explain all these behaviors is our overarching desire to be happy. Where the need to survive fails as an explanatory concept, the desire for happiness succeeds. For instance, deathbed confessions are motivated by the desire to feel good by unburdening oneself of evil-doing. Laughter is the discovery of not having to take seriously—feel bad—about what we thought we did. Grief, in the end, is the experience of believing we are good for feeling bad because it gives us the feeling of being close and caring. People who take religious vows or choose to do good want to be good and ultimately feel good. Celibacy, abortion,, voluntary childlessness, and homosexuality have nothing to with species survival and everything to do with the individuals' beliefs that their life choices will give them a happier existence. Finally, how can genes explain suicide? There can be no greater proof that survival theory has overreached because suicide is an act of self-destruction. Attempts have been made to show how individuals have sacrificed themselves for the survival of their families and social groups. Suicides are rarely motivated by such considerations. Except in the cases of religious and political self-immolation, suicides are convinced that they cannot be happy or at least not happy enough to continue to live. And so, what they are killing is their unhappiness. We do not strive to be happy in order to survive; we survive in order to be happy.

# 7

# Environment–The Historical Future

*Hear me, all of you, and try to understand. Nothing that enters a man from outside can make him impure; that which comes out of him and only that constitutes impurity.*

Mark 7:14–16

*Experience is not what happens to a man; it is what a man does with what happens to him.*

Aldous Huxley

*Nothing that is worth knowing can be taught.*

Oscar Wilde

*Scientists have not been able to discover many profound principles that relate the actions of mothers, fathers, or siblings to psychological characteristics of the child.*

Jerome Kagan

*All happy families are alike.*

Leo Tolstoy

*Don't look for the meaning; look for the use.*

Ludwig Wittgenstein

So far, we have seen that all the internal causal accounts of negative emotions have been found wanting. Although they all seem to be implicated, viscera, neurotransmitters, hormones, and genes can't account for why we become unhappy. So, except for the brain itself, which will be dealt with in the next chapter, the only other place to look for a causal account is externally, namely, the environment.

Nobody is born unhappy, because nobody is born with the full-blown self-awareness that allows us to put ourselves down. What babies are born with that mimics unhappiness is an innate startle reaction to certain environmental stimuli, such as sudden noises or being dropped. A baby's cry is not about being unhappy; it is how infants express their needs. As a colleague of mine used to say, babies cry because they can't whistle. It would be a mistake to equate the primitive reaction of a neonate with an adult emotion. That means that complex emotions like jealousy, embarrassment, and resentment are learned. Moreover, they are always associated with negative self-awareness, which was also learned. Although it is true that they originate in the environment, we have already established that the social environment alone is insufficient to cause us to feel negatively about ourselves. Yet, regardless of the level of intelligence, degree of sophistication, cultural background, ethnic origin, and family history, the overwhelming majority of people on planet Earth account in some way for their unhappiness as being caused by the environment. Some examples:

The other woman makes me *jealous*.

Cloudy days *depress* me.

I am *outraged* by injustice.

Successful people make me *envious*.

She *angers* me when she doesn't listen to me.

Dirty jokes *embarrass* me.

He *resented* his father's treatment of him.

The party *bored* me.

To be sure, there is interaction between the environment and the production of a negative feeling, but what is the nature of that relationship? It would appear to be simply an "if ... then" connection. All of our understanding of natural events is guided by this dynamic. If we prick a bubble, then it will burst; if we turn a key, then a door will open; if we step on the brake, then the car will stop and so on ad infinitum. It is this kind of thinking that has served us well in explaining natural phenomena. So why wouldn't that same explanation work with negative emotions? More important, why wouldn't it also account for our negative personal identity, which, as I have tried to show, is the real cause of negative emotions?

Using our first example of the "other woman" and its relationship to jealousy, it would appear to be simply a question of a cause preceding its effect, a stimulus preceding its response. Experience, logic, and for that matter, common sense would appear to back this explanation. The problem is that experience, logic, and common sense have it wrong. The failure to recognize the critical difference between an individual focusing on an environmental event and mistakenly believing it to be its cause has led most of humanity to embrace a pseudo-causal explanation of unhappiness known as a *post hoc fallacy*, which means *after this, therefore* or *because of this*. It describes the notion that since one event follows another, the preceding event caused the latter. To say that the other woman causes jealousy is as fallacious as saying that getting out of bed in the morning causes us to brush our teeth. What causes us to brush our teeth when we get out of bed is our belief that brushing will preserve our teeth, and what causes us to become jealous when we see or imagine the other woman is our belief that, among other things, we are inadequate. Many people would deny this explanation. The following diagram might best illustrate that most people believe that environmental events do, in fact, cause their unhappiness:

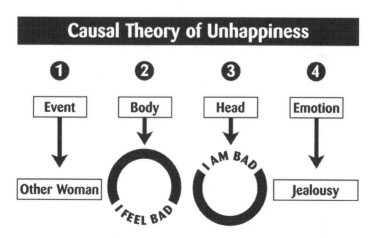

As you can see, in all explanations of emotions, the external event or stimulus appears first in the sequence. Although the sequence of events appears identical to the visceral model, the causal model is unique in several significant respects. Most important, unlike the visceral model, where the process is initiated by the percipient, the environment starts the sequence. Here, it is the selective process of the environment that acts on the individual. The belief that the person is "bad" or "defective"—which in my view is first—comes in dead last in the causal scheme, and we are reduced to the status of impotent bystanders in our own emotional lives. It doesn't help that this seemingly common-sense view of everyday experience is further bolstered by environmentalist psychologists, who play down internal influences and declare that the environment is the primary determinant of one's emotional life. B. F. Skinner, the most influential environmentalist of the twentieth century, believed, as stated earlier, that "the unhappy conditions of the world" are indeed the cause of our sad existence.

In earlier chapters, I also played down internal influences, arguing that viscera, genes, and psychoactive drugs were not the cause of negative feelings. Not even social situations themselves, which are environmental, could be the culprits. In every case, it was our negative self-perception in social situations that made us feel bad. However, not all environmental events would qualify as social situations. Might it not be possible that rainy days, seasonal adjustments, and other environmental intangibles influence our moods? Is it not possible that these non-social environmental events directly cause us to feel bad, without being filtered through how we see ourselves? An environmentalist would say yes, believing that even how we come to see ourselves is caused by the environment.

So what and how do we learn from the objects in our environment? We know that environmental objects always stay outside of us. So how did these external objects come to produce a personal history, which is inside us? Our modern way of expressing the answer is *conditioning*. That means that a rewarding situation increases the probability of a response (reinforcement), while a punishing situation decreases the probability of a response. In other words, the environment causes us to behave the way we do. Following this line of reasoning, the way we view ourselves is also just part of that reinforcing process. Jealous behavior is the result of a personal history created by repeated rejection.

The critical point is that a person cannot initiate anything. Behavior is completely controlled by a person's history of exposure to reinforcing stimuli in the environment. In this causal model, the relationship between the external stimulus and the person having the emotional response might be compared to the relationship of ragweed and an allergy sufferer. The ragweed in the environment only selects those who have a personal history of hay fever allergy, which in this biological context is probably genetic. Similarly, in a psychological context the "other woman" selects only those jealous individuals who have been made susceptible by virtue of their personal history, which was also the product of reinforcement.

Viewed this way, a woman whose boyfriend drops her for another woman becomes jealous in the here and now because she has already been conditioned to feel inadequate in the past, all of which is the product of environmental stimuli being stamped in and stamped out via rewards and punishment. The usually unspoken and unobservable subtext, *I'm not good enough,* is merely part of the behavioral package. Presumably, it is this unseen personal history that allows us to understand why it is that jealousy occurs when an external stimulus such as the "other woman" appears in our environment. This is how an environmentalist psychologist (aka behaviorist) would account for jealousy.

## Conditioning

Behaviorism, which focused exclusively on behavior, has been largely superseded by cognitive psychology, which focuses on internal mental states, which includes belief formation. Nevertheless, since behaviorism was a major school of thought and still has an influence on how people think about psychological matters, we should spend a little time trying to understand its point of view.

The most counterintuitive and least commonsensical aspect of behaviorism is its repudiation of introspection. Environmentalists believe that the question of what we do in our heads should be abandoned, and our focus should be only on what we can observe. Unlike neuroscientists (which we will focus on in the next chapter), who tend to demote conscious events to the status of afterthoughts, behaviorists tend to dismiss "mental" events altogether. They treat such unobservable issues like beliefs, desires, self-perception and emotions as just more behavior to be explained in terms of stimulus-response associations. For them, personal history is environmental history.

Although conditioning techniques might be seen as impressive when it comes to explaining simpler behaviors, it comes up dramatically short when applied how we see ourselves. The Harvard psychologist, Gordon Allport, a contemporary of Skinner with a comparable reputation, observed that reward and punishment—conditioning, if you will—cannot be applied to what he termed "ego-involved" activity. He showed that even repeated success at a task does not typically increase the probability of that same task being repeated, nor does persistent failure at a task necessarily decrease the probability of the same task being discontinued. For instance, when the ego (a term that I regard as equivalent to self-esteem) is involved, repeated success usually becomes boring. Repeated failure at a task often offers challenging opportunities for self-improvement and mastery.

This point of view also supports my experience, which is that when trying to account for how we come to view ourselves, repeated success or failure are largely irrelevant issues. Only a few of my clients who experience chronic jealousy have had a personal history of repeated rejection. Most came from average backgrounds and some have openly admitted that they had lives virtually free of rejection. There is usually nothing in their past environment or their present that could account for such a debilitating self-contemptuous emotion. As a marriage counselor, I've observed that in the overwhelming number of cases, the spouses of jealous partners are models of fidelity.

## Parental Love

Despite the fact that conditioning fails to explain how we see ourselves, dislodging baby-boomer parents from the belief that low self-esteem is always caused by uncaring or unloving parents is a formidable undertaking. In order to demonstrate that it is not the events themselves that constitute personal history, but rather how we choose to view those events, let's examine the following two case studies:

## Rejection

Setting:    Billy's mother came to see me about her precocious six-year-old son. She said that she felt inept and utterly helpless in the face of questions posed by him. As a former schoolteacher and having had experience teaching gifted children, I understood that they often ask disconcertingly incisive questions. Yet, since the mother appeared to be a woman of considerable intelligence, it seemed to me that she might be exaggerating the complexity of her son's inquiries. Judging by his opening question, she was not.

| | |
|---|---|
| Billy: | If God exists, why does he permit parents to stop loving you?[5] [He was referring to his father, who he accurately perceived had been indifferent to him for several months.] |
| PS: | Do you doubt the existence of God because your father stopped loving you, or because you felt bad about the fact that he stopped loving you? |
| Billy: | I doubt it, because only a cruel God would let that happen. |
| PS: | God's cruelty, I take it, refers to the fact that he is responsible for your feeling bad? |
| Billy: | Yes. |
| PS: | So God's goodness was only called into question because of your bad feeling? |
| Billy: | Yes. |
| PS: | And if you didn't feel bad, there would be no doubt as to God's existence—at least, on that account, and your problem would be solved. |
| Billy: | Yes. But how could I not feel bad if my father stops loving me? |
| PS: | Do you think it's possible? |
| Billy: | I'm not sure. |
| PS: | In any case, the solution to your problem would seem to be either to get your father to love you again, or to find a way for you not to feel bad if he doesn't. |
| Billy: | I tried over and over again to get him to pay attention to me the way he used to. I'll show him my science project that got an A-plus and he'll go, "My, A–plus, that's great," and hardly looks. |
| PS: | Then the only other solution is to help you to not feel bad, in spite of the fact that he is as unloving as you say. |

---

5    This question deals with the issue of *theodicy*, a subject argued by theologians for centuries. It deals with the problem of evil and in more conventional form, it poses the question: If God is God, He must be good. If He is not good, then He cannot be God.

| | |
|---|---|
| Billy: | I think that's going to be very hard to do. |
| PS: | Let's see. It would seem to be possible. Let's see if we can carry it out in practice. First off, can you think of anything that you did to cause your father to withdraw his love from you? |
| Billy: | I must have. Maybe I'm a disappointment to him. Maybe I'm not the kind of son he wanted. |
| PS: | Why do you believe that? |
| Billy: | The way he is. We were going out Saturday, but when I woke up, he had already left. He must not have wanted me to tag along. |
| PS: | You can't be sure of that. But there's one thing you can be sure of. |
| Billy: | What's that? |
| PS: | You can be sure that you never had any intention of losing your father's love. |
| Billy: | Yes, I'm sure of that. |
| PS: | And how does it feel to know that? |
| Billy: | Better. But I still can't be sure that I didn't do something accidentally. |
| PS: | You believe it is possible that you can accidentally prevent your father from loving you? |
| Billy: | It's possible. |
| PS: | How is that done? Could you give me an example? |
| Billy: | I could have done something he didn't like … like argue too much, and he didn't tell me about it. |
| PS: | If that were so, are you to be blamed that he didn't tell you? I'm sure if you'd known that, you might have tried discussing things with him without seeming to argue. |
| Billy: | I guess not. |
| PS: | How do you feel to know that? |
| Billy: | Better. |

| PS: | And if you know you never had any intention of alienating your father, then the only way he could withdraw from you would be to misinterpret your intentions. |
| Billy: | Yes. |
| PS: | How does it feel to know that? |
| Billy: | Better. But I'm still feeling bad. |
| PS: | Why? What are you afraid it would mean if you didn't feel bad? |
| Billy: | It would mean that I didn't love him. |
| PS: | Would it have to mean that? |
| Billy: | No, I guess not. |
| PS: | How do you feel knowing that? |
| Billy: | Good. But still, how would you explain why he doesn't seem to care about me anymore? |
| PS: | I guess we would have to ask him. |
| Billy: | Are you saying that the problem starts with him? |
| PS: | Where else? |

The scenario, as you can see, contains all the requisite elements: the where and when that are said to be the origins of emotional problems, including parental withdrawal, feelings of abandonment, helplessness in the face of rejection. If this interchange reached a happy conclusion, it did so by switching to a point of view that focuses on the child as interpreter and final arbiter in the world of unfolding events. In the end, it is the child who will agree that he or she is bad when that lesson is taught or conclude that they are bad even when it isn't.

## Resentment

In the case that follows, Rita's resentment was not the result of a parent's rejection, but quite the contrary. Incest is usually not a violent or an intentionally abusive act. Nonetheless, she also believed that she was to blame, which produces the same psychological result.

Setting: Rita is a thirty-two-year-old mother of two small children, who complains of sleeplessness and chronic anxiety. She feels she is heading for a breakdown. Although she has a good relationship with her husband,

and regards him as kind and loving, she sporadically experiences bouts of inexplicable resentment towards him.

| | |
|---|---|
| Rita: | If I get any unhappier than I already am, I think I will die. |
| PS: | What are you unhappy about? |
| Rita: | Everything. But perhaps I ought to start at the beginning. I understand that childhood events are important. Is it all right if I start there? |
| PS: | If you like. |
| Rita: | I know my problems have to do with the fact that I was sexually abused as a child. Between the ages of about eleven to thirteen, I had sexual relations with my father. |
| PS: | How is that related to your present problems? |
| Rita: | Well, isn't it? |
| PS: | I know that you think it is. |
| Rita: | How do you think I've become so resentful? |
| PS: | Would you like to get rid of your resentment? |
| Rita: | Just like that? |
| PS: | We can try. Let's start with your father, since that is where it seems to have begun. |
| Rita: | My father's image never leaves me. He's been dead for five years, and I hate him and resent him as much as ever. I think it's getting worse. It's even affecting my relationship with my husband. I feel helpless to change it. At least if I could stop resenting my husband, it would be a big help. |
| PS: | Who would you like to focus on first—your father or your husband? |
| Rita: | My father, I think. Does it matter? |
| PS: | Not really. |
| Rita: | Why not? |
| PS: | Because the rationale guiding the resentment is probably the same. In any case, no matter whom we focus on first, the problem before us is to eliminate your resentment. |

Rita: Then I'll never resolve my problem. I know my husband doesn't merit my treatment of him. But my father is another matter. I'll never stop resenting my father. There must be another way.

PS: I understand the reason for your resistance. On the face of it, it borders on the outrageous to suggest that you stop resenting your father.

Rita: I am absolutely justified. I've every right to loathe and detest him. My god, if my father couldn't be trusted, who can? I have two little girls, and whenever my husband physically handles them, I feel this awful anxiety and tension.

PS: Has he ever done anything to merit your suspicion?

Rita: No. But I am always on my guard. Like the nights he puts them to bed. And it's not just him. It extends to all men. There's an assistant manager at the supermarket, Hector. He lets my little girl help him make the pyramids of Jell-O; he tells her about his little girl, Nydia. I said to her, "Hector never tries to take you in the back of the store, does he?" She looked at me and said, "What for?" My paranoia even seeps into my friendships. One woman who's divorced has a split-custody arrangement. I said to her, "You mean you let her go and stay with him?" and she said, "Well, what on earth could he do to her?" Do you know, when all the daycare scandals were in the news, I was kind of relieved. I felt as if I could say, "See? Now the truth is coming out." That's how ingrained my attitude is. I can't imagine it changing.

PS: Yes, you can; you're talking to me. That tells me you believe change is possible.

Rita: I guess so.

PS: I'm glad you see that. So let's not waste any time. One minute of unhappiness is one minute too long. Are there times in your experience when you are relaxed about the safety of your children?

Rita: Never completely relaxed. When I start to be, something jars me. Like, my little girl was on my husband's lap for a bedtime story, and she accidentally grabbed his thigh high up, and he jumped a little, and I said "Oh, don't hurt poor Daddy." That's how I put it. Or, we were walking into the supermarket, and I was thinking, *Hector is a sweet young man,* and he was crouched down, stocking the lower shelves, and she ran up behind him and covered his eyes to "guess who." I said, "Oh, don't scare poor Hector!" and he said, "Oh, she doesn't bother me!" But I tell you; a kind of shock that went through me that she could feel so bold with him.

PS: But sometimes you're more relaxed than at other times? Like when you thought of Hector as a nice young man.

Rita: Yes.

PS: At those times, there must be something you're doing or not doing that allows that to happen. When you're comparatively relaxed—isn't it true that you're less resentful at those times?

Rita: Yes.

PS: So as long as you are resenting your father or anyone else for that matter, nothing will change. Is there anything preventing you from not resenting your father?

Rita: I can't do that. It would be tantamount to forgiving him.

PS: But he's dead. You're forgiving him doesn't benefit him, but it does relax you.

Rita: I can't forgive him.

PS: What does it mean to forgive someone?

Rita: It means that what he did was all right.

PS: Would not resenting him necessarily imply that you forgive him?

Rita: I guess not.

PS: Will you stop resenting him?

82

| | |
|---|---|
| Rita: | I can't. |
| PS: | Okay. Let's look at it from another point of view. Tell me, did you resent him from the very start? |
| Rita: | What do you mean? |
| PS: | Do you recall when you started feeling resentful over what he was doing? |
| Rita: | I really started to feel awful later on. I guess when I found out my girlfriends' fathers weren't doing it. |
| PS: | And if you never found out what you were doing was out of the normal, would you have ever gotten resentful? |
| Rita: | What are you getting at? |
| PS: | Only that you started resenting your father after you found what he was doing was abnormal. |
| Rita: | It was, and he was a degenerate! |
| PS: | Did you think you were a degenerate for letting him? |
| Rita: | I didn't let him. |
| PS: | Did he force you? |
| Rita: | [Sobs] No. Are you saying I'm to blame? |
| PS: | Not at all. That's what you are saying about yourself. It might interest you to know that these things are rarely coercive. In any case, you allowed him to do it, and you won't forgive yourself for having done so. Self-forgiveness is the real solution to your problem. |
| Rita: | How do I forgive myself? |
| PS: | By simply recognizing the reason that you allowed him have sex with you, and realizing that it was a not bad reason. |
| Rita: | What was the reason? |
| PS: | I think you know. Think; why did you let him? |
| Rita: | I was afraid he would be angry with me if I didn't do as he asked. I was afraid he wouldn't love me anymore. You seemed to know what I was going to say. |

| | |
|---|---|
| PS: | Yes, because something like that is usually the reason. You did it so as not to alienate your father. Is that a bad reason? |
| Rita: | I guess not. |
| PS: | Is there anything still stopping you from relaxing about this whole matter? |
| Rita: | Yes, I think so. |
| PS: | Suppose you stopped feeling bad; what do you fear would happen? |
| Rita: | I'd let my guard down, and I might not be alert about the safety of my children. |
| PS: | You believe that if you relaxed, your children would be less protected? |
| Rita: | They might. |
| PS: | Would they? |
| Rita: | Perhaps not. |
| PS: | Are you more relaxed now? |
| Rita: | Yes. |
| PS: | Are your children any less protected? |
| Rita: | I see what you mean. |

For decades, the power of parental power to disesteem has reigned as the decisive explanation as to why we are so troubled. In the nineteenth century, Jean Jacques Rousseau, the man who did the most to promote the importance of parental love, decreed it as the panacea that would produce happy adults. He successfully convinced the Western world that the ills of society are traceable to unloving parents. In the twentieth century, most developmental psychologists and therapists also professed an unshakable belief in the power of parental love to create a bond during the first three years of life that was to head off later psychological problems.

In reaction to this dogma of parental love, John B. Watson, the father of American behaviorism, in his influential 1928 handbook, *Psychological Care of Infant and Child,* stated, "Never hug and kiss them, never let them sit in your lap. If you must, kiss them once on the forehead when they say good night. Shake hands with them in the morning." The U.S. government

Department of Health, Education and Welfare handbook of the 1920s instructed nursing mothers to lie on the bed alongside the infant, to avoid touching them, to change breasts, get up and lie on the baby's other side.

Since then, all kinds of reactions and counter-reactions to prescriptions on raising children have followed. Experts may reverse themselves, argue with other experts on such perennial issues as the emotional risks of weaning too early or too late, of too much or too little praise, of picking up or not picking up a crying baby, of parents divorcing or staying together for the kids, of surrogate care, environmental enrichment, and so on. Child rearing appears to be dictated by what theory is in fashion and who is selected as the reigning expert at the time. If we remain more or less in the dark as to just what constitutes the best possible childcare methods, it's because all research on child development presumes that since there are certain factors that have been shown to have a bearing on physical development and growth, there must be a similar set of factors involved in psychological and emotional growth.

As to the physical development of the child, we know that infants who are physically handled grow faster and bigger. That can be measured. But we also know that it hardly matters who the handler is, or even whether the stimulation is unpleasant or gentle. We also know that feral children—who grow up without human contact—will be linguistically and emotionally compromised and will never interact normally in social situations. Apparently, there is a maturational window of opportunity that, when missed, makes complete remediation impossible.

But as to the psychological and emotional development of the typical child brought up where there is human contact, there are no known stimulants that can measure psychological and emotional growth. What that means is that, psychologically speaking, there are no *nurturants;* there are only *interpretants,* only events that a child will or will not agree to as evidence for its being defective. This forces us to reconsider what we mean by "parental love."

## The Child as Historian

One of the more compelling studies in recent times having to do with this issue was reported by Jerome Kagan in his book, *The Nature of the Child.* While working with the Mayan Indians of northwest Guatemala, he showed that Mayan mothers who labor in the fields, leaving their infants hanging suspended in hammocks in the darkness of a shed for long hours during the day in order to protect them from the sun and animals, nonetheless produced children who became psychologically sound as they matured. He concludes, "Scientists have not been able to discover many profound principles that relate the actions of mothers, fathers, or siblings to psychological characteristics in the child."

I don't mean to suggest that mothers in different socioeconomic situations ought to emulate the child rearing style of Mayan mothers. In our country, mothers who hung their children in hammocks on hooks while they worked would be arrested for child abuse. Nevertheless, it ought to be stated that with all the clamor about, for example, environmental enrichment, no convincing evidence has ever been adduced to justify its vaunted benefits. The reason for this is that the ideas found in Rousseau and Watson and everything in between and since have focused on the events surrounding the child and their putative causal influence, while failing to appreciate that we have no final control as to how these events will be processed. Since not everyone responds the same way to environmental events, personal history can't equate to environmental history. There must be something inside us that makes that variation possible. The selective process as to how we see ourselves must be something *we* do and not what the environment does.

It is undeniable that self-deprecation is learned early in life, and that it is the substrate out of which a negative personal identity is created. Even if it were argued that in the early developmental stages that the naiveté of children would predispose them to believe what the significant members of their narrow social world want them to believe, it is also true that not everything that is taught is learned, nor is everything that is learned retained. If teaching guaranteed learning, every school system would be unfailingly successful. Parents and educators may want to teach, but ultimately it is the children who decide what they come to believe. I think that Oscar Wilde surmised this when he said, "Nothing that is worth knowing can be taught." So while a negative self-perception is more likely to occur in an unloving family, it is also clear that not all emotionally troubled adults come from abusive families. Neither do abusive families necessarily produce emotionally troubled adults. Despite the fact that there is no objective standard for what constitutes too much or too little love, loving parents are still widely regarded as the one certain prophylaxis against later emotional disturbance. If "the child is father to the man" means that the beliefs we acquire as a child shape us as adults, then the understanding of how we acquire those beliefs cannot be modeled on the physical sciences, whose investigative points of departure focus on the where and when of things.

What we should take away from this is that family history is an unbroken continuum of evolving time. Personal history is what we abstract from that unbroken continuum. Reconstructing history is not simply the result of cataloging events. It is done by making selections from a countless array of past events. The child, *as historian,* not only selects certain events to the exclusion of others, those chosen events themselves are a series of interpretations. Those choices are what produce a personal identity. Regardless of one's family background, the child, as interpreter, must never be underestimated. That is why, when talking about personal identity and the psychology of emotions, historical explanations of how human beings acquire beliefs cannot be based on understanding the initial conditions that presumably led to the end result, what we normally refer to as the past. This sort of awareness was powerfully implied in the play, *Equus,* by Peter Schaffer. The protagonist, Dysart, a dedicated psychiatrist grappling with the origin of his patient's psychological difficulty, speaks these words:

> *A child is born into a world of phenomena all equal in their power to enslave. It sniffs—it sucks—it strokes its eyes over the whole uncountable range. Suddenly one strikes. Why? Moments snap together like magnets, forging a chain of shackles. Why? I can trace them. I can even, with time, pull time apart again. But why at the start they were ever magnetized at all—Just those moments of experience and no others—I don't know. And nor does anyone else [author's emphasis]. Yet if I don't know—if I can never know that— then what am I doing here? I don't mean clinically doing or socially doing—I mean fundamentally? These questions, these whys are fundamental—yet they have no place in a consulting room. So then, do I?*

Dysart's realization that neither he nor anyone else can ever know the origin of an emotional problem is not a face-saving rationalization from someone who lacks skill. He recognizes the fundamental fallacy inherent in environmental explanations of events involving human participants. Perhaps this is what the psychiatrist David Abrams, testifying as an expert witness in the Son of Sam trial, had in mind when he said, "What the hell do psychiatrists know anyhow?"

Ludwig Wittgenstein, arguably the most original and influential English speaking philosopher of the twentieth century, wisely reminded us "Don't look for meaning; look for its use." When we understand that beliefs are learned because of their perceived usefulness and not because they are taught, the where and when recede in importance in the process of "getting to the bottom of things." Regardless of the environmental surroundings, youngsters have a choice as to what they come to believe. They may decide that staying within the mainstream of accepted middle-class values gives them social acceptance, a good retirement, and a longer, healthier life. Put differently, they accept middle-class values, because they may want to avoid isolation, impoverishment, and a shorter, less healthy life. Others may believe that obeying the rules is wimpy, that living on the edge is useful for a more exciting life. They may want to avoid boredom, stultification, or mediocrity. Those beliefs might produce a personal identity of an entrepreneur, an adventurer, or a criminal. For those who insist on the causal influence of the where and when of one's environmental history, it annoys them no end when children who later become serial murderers are found not to have had horrific childhoods. The serial killers, Jeffrey Dahmer and Ted Bundy, from all accounts, had unremarkable family backgrounds. That means that regardless of the open or closed nature of one's family background, despite one's loving or loveless family life, the renegade cannot be prevented from coming into being. The recalcitrant, be he saint, criminal, genius, or simple non-believer, will always live among us.

One of the most impassioned defenses of this point of view can be found by returning to the play, *Equus:*

> *Let me tell you something. We are not criminals. We've done nothing wrong. We loved Alan. We gave him the best love we could. All right, we quarrel sometimes—all parents quarrel—we always make it up. My husband is a good man. He's an upright man, religion or no religion. He cares for his home, for the world, and for his boy. Alan had love and care and treats, and as much fun as any boy in the world. I know about loveless homes. I was a teacher. Our home wasn't loveless. I know about privacy too—and invading a child's privacy. All right, Frank may be at fault there—he digs into him too much—but nothing in excess. He's not a bully ...*
> *No Doctor.* Whatever's happened has happened because

> of Alan *[ author's emphasis]. Alan is himself. Every soul is
> itself. If you added up everything we ever did to him, from
> his first day on earth to this, you wouldn't find why he did
> this terrible thing[6]—because that's him: not all of our things
> added up. Do you understand what I'm saying? I want you to
> understand, because I lie awake and awake thinking it out,
> and I want you to know that I deny it absolutely, what he's
> doing now, staring at me, attacking me for what he's done,
> for what he is …*

The case has to be made that even parents who have been steadfast in their love may have their efforts summarily dismissed by their child. It has also been demonstrated that so-called protective parents are sometimes unwittingly led into that role by very demanding children. Parental love, how ever desirable, and parental indifference, how ever undesirable, still require the child's interpretation in the world of unfolding events. The environmental circumstances—the past, if you will—only provides the context within which the *moments of experience* are extracted to create a personal history. This lack of understanding about why children learn what they do and the insistence on the all-powerful causal influence of external events has only succeeded in confusing the most assiduous parents. "Am I marking him or her for life?" has become a chronic cultural anxiety that has not only taken a good deal of the joy out of being a parent; it has also led to confusion, excuse-making, and indecisiveness.

Ironically, the truly neglectful parent is never troubled by such a question and is certainly not known to ever pick up a book on parenting. When children act uncooperatively, it leads parents to make silly disingenuous statements like, "I love you, but I don't like you." When parents feel compelled to make that kind of distinction, they invariably do so because they either feel responsible in some way for the behavior that they observe or feel that they are bad for noticing it. Neither is true. We ought not trick ourselves into believing that people are not defined by their behavior, because it makes us look and feel like liars, and it induces the other not to change. Parents ought never to see their children as victims when they are denied, nor be put off by their children's less-than-willing cooperation. The true parenting experts ought never doubt the goodness of their intentions. They need to understand what they can control and what they can't, that their love for their child can be trusted to guide their choices and, in the

---

6    The teenage character blinded six horses.

end, the child will decide whether he or she will be grateful or not. Tolstoy said, "All happy families are alike." At the risk of being presumptuous, I'd like to think that he might have agreed with this analysis.

In the quotations that head this chapter, Jesus (through Mark) and Aldous Huxley clearly declared themselves not to be environmentalists. Twentieth-century psychology, however, has placed Jesus and Huxley in a minority position. In any case, whether the idea that we alone are the cause of our unhappiness is presented as a spiritual truth by a sublime soul or the astute observation of a first-rate intellectual, it is what we first did in our head and how we focus on the objects of the world that causes our unhappiness, not the other way around. "The kingdom of God is within you," whether understood as a religious pronouncement or a psychological truth, is still excellent counsel. But before we give a full psychological account of what takes place within us that prevents us from entering *the kingdom*, we must examine the last possible place to look for a causal explanation for unhappiness—the brain.

# 8

# The Brain–Not To Be Confused With Mind

*If evolution is to work smoothly, consciousness, in some shape, must have been present at the very origin of things.*
William James.

*The brain does not function as a single-area organ.*
Rodolfo Llimas

*The hallmark of consciousness is a non-algorithmic forming of judgments.*
Roger Penrose

*The brain may not be capable, in the last analysis, of providing an explanation of itself.*
Gunther Stent

*Absence of evidence is not evidence of absence.*
Carl Sagan

*We don't even have bad ideas.*
Noam Chomsky

An ancient notion, still very much alive, is the concept of *soul which, simply* defined, is a personal identity, a sort of essence of personality, a spiritual self within the material world but not governed by it. As defined by *The Merriam-Webster Dictionary,* the soul is "the immaterial essence of an individual life ... the spiritual principle embodied in human beings ...

an active or essential part [of] the moral and emotional nature of human beings." The ancient Greeks believed that the exact location of the soul was not in the brain but in the liver. Two thousand years later, the philosopher, Rene Descartes, saw the idea of the soul as a creation of God, a more divine aspect of self, which he believed served as the liaison between mind and body. Unlike the Greeks, Descartes put the soul not in the liver but in the pineal gland, located in the center of the brain.

Over the centuries, ever since Descartes opened the mind-body can of worms, this troublesome issue has been worked over in a variety of ingenious ways. It has been said that science has made no significant progress investigating consciousness. Noam Chomsky commented in this regard, "We don't even have *bad* ideas." Some materialists try to get around this is by denying anything that is "mental." They believe that whatever happens in our brains is simply a rearrangement of sensation patterns. Others believe that the brain "secretes" thought. Some believe that Descartes had it right; i.e., the mind affects the body. Still others claim that the body can also affect the mind. Finally, there are those who claim that there is no physical reality at all other than the mental realm that resides within. This last position is called *panpsychism*.

In its more modern formulation, panpsychists propose that it is *protoconsciousness*–a universal intelligence —not matter, that is the pervasive stuff of the universe. In the movie *2001,* the sudden appearance of a black monolith among the evolving primates represents this point of view. The theory goes that all matter, including subatomic particles, contains consciousness. The reasoning is that it would be impossible for a complex information and communication system like the brain to pop up out of nowhere. Since the brain is made up of the same constituent parts that make up the rest of the world, these subatomic elements must also contain some bits of consciousness. Some more cautiously prefer to use the term *mentation,* the process of thinking itself, but in either case, brain, in the evolutionary scheme of things, is only an elaboration and refinement of the consciousness that exists in all matter, albeit a more complex organization of consciousness. The higher the animal, not measured by the size of the brain but by weight ratio between the brain and the spinal cord, the larger and more developed the consciousness.

Needless to say, none of these theories have been shown to be definitive. Nor do any of them settle the immediate question of a possible neural location in the brain, which would give rise to self-consciousness, let alone negative self-consciousness.

In the last century, an enormous amount has been learned about the brain. There are many psychological conditions that do match up very well with specific physiological areas in the brain. A condition known as temporal lobe focal epilepsy is characterized by rage and, sometimes, homicidal behavior. It is caused by a calcified mass in the temporal lobe. When the mass is removed, the behavior ceases. If a certain area in the right hemisphere is destroyed, laughter becomes impossible. Brain anatomists have located specific neural locations in the brain that control speech, movement, comprehension, and many other functions. Electrical stimulation of specific areas in the brain can increase or decrease appetite, and there are pleasure centers in the brain that respond to electrical stimulation. With all this impressive research, neuroscientists might reasonably believe that all emotional experiences are derived from neural mechanisms, that all conscious experiences are a reflection of brain activities.

Their materialistic way of thinking established the theoretical justification for treating the brain—or some other part of the body—in order to heal the mind. In the early part of the twentieth century, this approach led to medical remedies such as hydrotherapy, the fever cure, insulin-coma therapy, the sleep cure, and the administering of powerful emetics and laxatives. Other therapies consisted of the surgical removal of various body parts, such as gonads, ovaries, colons, thyroids, and other glands. Unnecessary hysterectomies were performed on women because it was believed that hysteria was a disease emanating from the womb. All of these approaches were not only worthless, they violated the fundamental admonition of the Hippocratic oath—"First do no harm."

Later contenders, which could not have emerged as treatment modalities had it not been for the doctrine of materialism, are psychosurgery, electroshock, and psychopharmacology. Their record of accomplishment is mixed to say the least. Psychosurgery has mostly disappeared as a creditable approach to solving "mental" disorders. We have seen the tragic legacy of those who have had lobotomies. Electroshock (ECT), though more humanely and prudently administered, has become the court of last resort after psychotherapy and drugs fail. When effective, the relief usually lasts about four months. For the last twenty five years psychopharmacology has held the field in the treatment of mental disorders by material means. If the materialists are right and microscopic activity in the cells of the brain is the source of our emotional problems, the responsibility for our unhappiness is essentially out of our hands. The role of consciousness in general and self-consciousness in particular becomes passive, just so much froth on a wave. Their claim is that feelings and negative perceptions of the world and of ourselves are *caused* by neural mechanisms in the brain that, in some as yet undiscovered way, have been disturbed by the environment. The materialists claim that if these approaches have not yet delivered on their promise of a cure, it will be just be a matter of time until new discoveries will allow them to do so. Unhappiness, they suggest, is a disorder that can be treated. This position is known as *eliminative materialism* because it eliminates the existence of most mental states, including common sense. Some, like the distinguished philosopher of science Karl Popper, have more disparagingly called it "promissory" materialism.

## Who Am I, Where Am I?

In the extraordinarily complex process of how we come to perceive anything, let alone ourselves, we should begin our analysis of how we perceive simpler, more visually concrete, objects in our environment. What has brain research discovered in the area of visual perception? More appropriately, what has *not* been discovered? No neurons have ever been found that would be useful in the reconstruction of a perceived image. There is no specific location in the brain that correlates with what we see. The optic nerve, which we associate with seeing, merely transmits visual information, not perception per se. What has been facetiously called the "grandmother cell" has not been discovered. There is no fixed set of neurons that are fired when we recognize that our grandmother has come into view. Even if more research found fixed neuronal connection between an observation and its object, it still wouldn't change anything as regards our happiness.

If homo sapiens, the knowing human, has not discovered a fixed set of neurons for perceiving concrete objects in the environment, which is, by comparison, a much simpler phenomenon than perception of self, what are the chances of a self-reflective homo sapiens, those who know that they know, discovering a fixed set of neurons called *the self*? Let's say for the sake of argument that our so-called individuality, the *I,* one's sense of self, is a linguistic invention, a fluke of grammar. How can such a faith-based assertion, which is nothing more than a sterile opinion really, add to the conversation about why we might be unhappy? What would it change? Nothing. How ever we choose to characterize or categorize the status of "self," it would remain impossible to conduct our lives without it.

As it presently stands, with all the modern sophisticated methods of brain research and imaging, the site of self-consciousness is nowhere to be found, and it is likely to stay that way. The *I* has no precise, spatiotemporal location within the brain. This poses a question of unimaginable complexity and, it would seem, beyond the pale of further brain research, because how can we explain an activity of something we can't even find? To soulists, the failure to uncover the self may be interpreted as a vindication of what they have always believed, namely, that the soul cannot be described in traditionally materialistic terms. For those who want to stay clear of the supernatural overtones of *soul,* a view closer to the natural order of explanation, although untraditional, may have more appeal to speak of *mind.* The near autonomy of the self to float limitlessly, to conjecture, combine, and separate without being tied to a fixed group of neurons in the brain or even to real people and events external to it can be made intelligible if we allow this speculation: Beyond a certain level of complexity a qualitative difference occurs. Non-linear, unstable dynamic phenomena like earthquakes or forest fires, for example, are synergistic reactions where the whole becomes greater than and different from the sum of its parts, and cannot be explained in the same way as other natural phenomena are understood. Consciousness is no less complex? If we dissect the brain, will that tell us what we need to know about consciousness? Clearly, the mind is not equivalent to the brain.

Roger Sperry, a Nobel laureate and neuroscientist, speaks of "downward causation." He suggests that when science deals with simple phenomena, it proceeds by reducing the whole into its component parts. It assumes that the key to explaining the whole is to be found in understanding its smaller units. This is known as "upward causation." On the other hand, consciousness, unlike all other phenomena, downwardly determines the fate of its component parts. Consciousness does not replace these electrochemical events; it supersedes them. Self-consciousness, the most complex unity of all, is not an incidental effect that occurs after the brain has done its work, like a by-product of smoke from a factory. It is, rather, an emergent property of the brain's processes, the explanatory causal construct, made of the parts it controls with its own laws and dynamics. In other words, the mind is in charge of the brain, not the reverse. This account would provide us with a sound theoretical basis for the existence of free will.

## Free Will and the Brain

Donald MacKay, a physicist, philosopher, and neuroscientist from England, notes that science proceeds by assuming that things exist and behave because an orderly set of prior events had to occur in order for an event under study to have happened. Specifying those events is what scientists do. The logic therein is that if we could specify all the antecedent conditions surrounding whatever we were studying, we would be able to predict with absolute certainty what would happen. That is no longer believed to be true. On the sub-microscopic levels of observation, quantum mechanics and the uncertainty principle have shown that complete specification of those prior events is impossible.

Nonetheless, the belief in complete specification is still a very serviceable way of doing science *macroscopically*. On the everyday level of observation, scientists never challenge the assumption that an orderly set of prior events are specifiable, that, in principle, they are completely specifiable. But, MacKay points out, it is never true with the brain. Even if brain scientists had a full account of how brain-cell activity was programmed, they would not be able to predict behavior with certainty. Suppose a scientist said he was in possession of all the specifiable neuronal events in your brain that would allow him to predict that you will play tennis Saturday morning at 9:00 AM. In principle, that is possible. Now, suppose the scientist told the tennis player about his prediction. The tennis player would be perfectly free to do otherwise. She could accept the prediction as correct or reject it as mistaken. The scientist would then say she would have to include that possibility in order to complete his specifications. But if that specification implicitly requires that the tennis player accept the prediction, then the scientist can never have a complete specification of prior events. If the scientist does not disclose his prediction to the tennis player, his prediction could hold because he has complete specifications of prior events. But if he *does* disclose it, complete specification becomes impossible, because it depends on whether or not the tennis player accepts the prediction. It is predictable, but not inevitable. The upshot of all this is that it makes people personally responsible for their behavior. It places the concept of free will and choice on a sound logical and scientific foundation.

The notion of free will has gotten impressive support from recent brain research. A process known as mind sculpting or *self-directed neuroplasticity*, has demonstrated that the brain can change as a result of the thoughts we think. Brain physiologists have also discovered an area within the brain that would appear to establish a sound, neurological basis for believing that consciousness exerts causal control over feelings and behavior. Sir John Eccles, a Nobel Prize laureate and neuroscientist, had probably done more than anyone to popularize a discovery known as the supplemental motor area. The SMA is a thin layer of cortical tissue located on the top of the brain. Its distinctive feature is that it is the only area of the brain discovered to be receptive to mental intentions leading to voluntary actions. SMA is not triggered by some other nerve cell; the discharges first occur in the SMA. This amounts to neurological evidence for free will.

The most recent attempt on the part of materialists to dismiss free will or choice from human affairs comes from computer science and the artificial intelligence community. The old materialist view, which viewed the plasticity of the brain as virtually infinite, likening it to a tape recorder where the environment recorded itself on a blank tape, was replaced by the computer paradigm. And just as the computer whose internal organization is programmed to work over external input, environmental input is supposed to be processed by the internal architecture of the brain.

The theory has been criticized by the mathematical physicist Roger Penrose and others, who have stated that computers can never emulate human thinking. Human brains can do a lot more than compute. Penrose concludes that "the hallmark of consciousness is a non-algorithmic forming of judgments." Belief formation and other conscious states are not reflex-like responses to the environment or produced by computer-like thinking, nor are they merely the product of the intricate neural networks of the brain itself. Consciousness operates by something more than a fixed set of rules. In addition to common sense, intuition, and insight, all conscious states possess *qualia,* a first-person, subjective quality of mind that is colored by some mood or other. It is what we mean when we *experience* something. It is the essential difference between computers and people. For example, computers move chess pieces, but people *play* chess. This is the acknowledged hard problem that neuroscientists will probably never solve—how subjective experience arises from neural computation.

Furthermore, it has been proposed by Sperry, among others, that brain function is innately goal-oriented and value-guided. Beliefs are the product of formed judgments. The material brain serves only as the necessary medium for self-consciousness to arise. Negative self-judgment, when it occurs, is not the product of something stored in the brain, but rather the consequence of the overall self-system of organization spread among the cells of the brain.

An analogy: water is the medium without which swimming could not take place, but water's presence can neither force someone to swim, nor cause him to decide whether he is good at it or not. Likewise, the brain is the medium without which self-reflection would be impossible, but it does not force you to focus on yourself and, even less, it can't cause you to determine whether you will like what you see or not.

The fact that neuroscience has failed to turn up any specific location in the brain that could account for the self or beliefs about the self lends itself to several possible conclusions. The soulist can view this as confirmation for the existence of the spiritual "soul." For the materialists, who are uncomfortable with supernatural or expanded notions of what ought to be included as natural explanations that same lack of evidence would serve to corroborate their stated view that all conscious experience is indeed illusory and hopelessly inconsistent with natural law. Specific locations in the brain have not been found because there is nothing to find. Construed in these terms, it is understandable why materialists might describe a conscious experience in the matter-energy world as "ghost talk." Oddly, if the non-material nature of mentalistic entities and the fact that such conscious entities have no discoverable spatiotemporal location in the brain confirms their position, it also confirms ours, since one of our main points has been to show that there are no external or internal causes of negative states. (Cause implies the movement of matter through space and time.) "Ghosts" would, therefore, be a most appropriate designation for uncaused, spaceless, and massless entities.

We might further agree with the materialists that the best way to handle ghosts is to reject them as unsuitable scientific material. So it would serve no useful purpose to further probe genes, viscera, biochemistry, or the brain in the hope of translating these ephemera into materialistic language. We might dismiss them altogether very much in the same manner that we dispatched witches and devils in centuries past. We did not do this by continuing to examine the body for a witch's mark or supernumerary nipples, for example, and refining our techniques for detecting and exorcising witches and devils. It was accomplished by the enlightened recognition that such mythological fictions were fumbling, unscientific attempts that failed to explain unconventional behavior and what those in power regarded as deviant psychological states. There is nothing preventing us from dismissing, in an equally unceremonious way, other spectral creations like the material basis for negative beliefs and thoughts about the self.

But that is not likely to happen, because even if we were to agree that the matter-energy world is a closed system that makes inadmissible any phenomenon that does not conform to the materialistic order as conventionally understood, ghosts are no less psychologically real for being so. Ghosts are no less haunting for being illusions. Witches, when believed in, will bewitch, and devils will bedevil, in spite of the fact that they are ruled out of court by materialists. They might counter that the only thing observable about illusory beliefs is the verbal behavior of those describing them. They are only verbal reports, and further, those who are reporting them could be lying. But then we would have to ask why people lie and then behave as if the lie were true.

We might agree that what people say they experience does not establish the existence of the experience. For the sake of argument, we might even sympathize with the materialists who will not accept anything that can't be observed, which is to say any phenomenon that can neither be verified nor falsified. We will accept their ground rules.

Let's begin then with what *is* observable: the existence of people who claim to experience what the materialists would doubtlessly characterize as their phantasmagoria. In any case, the counterfeit, be it illusion or lie, is observed, verbal behavior and, as such, requires an explanation. Fictional inventions have to be accounted for. The problem is that any explanation worthy of its name must invoke some notion of cause, but we have already ruled out all the possible causal explanations of unhappiness.

So let's take a closer look at the nature of causality.

# 9

# Causality–Pitchfork Or Carrot

*Why should there not be a psychological regularity to which no physiological regularity corresponds? If this upsets our concept of causality, then it is high time that it was upset.*

Ludwig Wittgenstein

*The most fundamental fact about us is that we have interests and purposes.*

Ludwig Wittgenstein

*They are not jealous for the cause, but they are jealous because they are jealous.*

William Shakespeare

Our reliance on cause is unavoidable. Anything that happens has a cause. Finding it is central to whatever we are trying to understand, especially our problem solving efforts. Granted, this can be a slippery concept, regardless of the problem we set our minds to because, strictly speaking, only correlations can be observed, not causality. For example, we observe that the sun rising in the east has always been followed by its setting in the west but we cannot conclude that one event caused the other. All we can reasonably claim is that one event is always followed by another, not that there is a transfer of something from a cause to an effect. Nevertheless, for our purposes, we still have to invoke the notion of causality if we have any hope in trying to understand unhappiness. The first thing to know about causality is that contained within it is the idea of uniformity–similar causes will produce similar effects. For example, here on earth, dropped objects (cause) fall to the ground (effect). Cause pays great attention to what should be excluded. Personal factors like the attitude, physical characteristics, nationality, and gender of the person dropping the object, along with an infinite number of environmental factors like where and when it was dropped, would be regarded as extraneous. It is also necessary to understand that causality does not allow for exceptions in the sequence of events. If the object fell in slow motion or suddenly stopped and hung suspended in midair, these exceptions would have to be explained within the existing body of scientific knowledge. If the exceptional case could not be explained, then the law of gravity would have to be repealed, or at least demoted to the status of a theory. In order for something to be truly causal, it is not enough that an environmental event *may* result in a negative feeling, it *must*.

True causes are exceptionless explanations of how one event necessarily follows another. Although the classical understanding of causality has been and continues to be quite serviceable on our everyday level of experience, with the advent of quantum mechanics, the notion of causality on the micro level doesn't work very well. Neither, as we have discovered, has the search for causality in psychological matters worked out very well. All the causal attempts to explain unhappiness proved to be inadequate because all our explorations were rife with exceptions.

Despite this, professional investigators still share the conviction that emotional problems are indeed caused by the subtle interaction among genetic, cultural, biochemical, and environmental factors. How this "subtle interaction" takes place is still anybody's guess. Still, it is the sort of catchall statement one can expect to read in all psychological textbooks. Close examination of this seemingly irrefutable statement reveals that it is content-free and barren. One would be hard-put to find any instance of human behavior that this assertion does not cover. Since it includes everything and excludes nothing, it fails spectacularly as a causal explanation. Lest you think that this criticism is overdrawn, consider these relationships:

| Causal Complaint | Focus | Examples |
|---|---|---|
| I feel bad because of | something that exists in one's current setting | any actual event, person, place, or thing |
| I feel bad because of what happened | something that existed in the past | any personal memory |
| I feel bad because of what will happen | something that will exist in the future | death, old age |
| I feel bad because there is no | something that is non-existent | God, justice, fun |
| I feel bad because of what might happen | something that exists as possibility | oblivion, loneliness, illness, failure |
| I feel bad because of the unknown | something that is nameless | non-reactive depression, free-floating anxiety, nothing-in-particular moods |
| I feel bad because I already have what I want | something that is in one's possession | success, money, baby (postpartum depression) |

What is clear from viewing this table is that there is literally nothing that exists or does not exist, in the present or in the past, nothing that will or might exist in the future, nothing real or imagined, desired or undesired, named or nameless, in or out of this world that cannot be used as a "cause" of feeling bad. And finally, even the external objects that we have yearned and striven for and that are in our possession can be seen as a cause of feeling bad. If knowledge is to be judged against how far human beings have come in narrowing the conditions under which unhappiness is made possible, then we are still at the point of absolute ignorance, because we have succeeded in excluding nothing. Not only have we not come a jot closer to eliminating possible causes, we have enlarged the list. Problems of alienation, dehumanization, and identity are relatively recent additions to the inventory of human discontent. The original *Diagnostic and Statistical*

*Manual of Mental Disorders (DSM),* published in 1952, contained sixty disorders. The current edition contains some three hundred.

Editions are regularly updated to include new disorders. Post-traumatic stress disorder (PTSD), attention deficit disorder (ADD), antisocial personality disorder (APD), and narcissistic personality disorder (NPD) are among the more familiar ones, but there are others. Among the more recent candidates are dissociative fugue disorder (DFD), seasonal adjustment (or affective) disorder (SAD), road rage disorder (RRD) and sudden wealth disorder (SWD), all of which have been traced to the new enemy—modernity and its offspring of technology, bigness, and whatever else social scientists will doubtlessly speculate about in the future. This means that as long as everything can be invoked as a possible cause of feeling bad, we have, in effect, stripped the concept of "cause" of any generally accepted meaning. To put it crudely, when everything can be the cause, then nothing is.

That is why there are, at last count, some 450, if not distinct, then overlapping schools of therapy and treatment. All manner of non-talk therapies have been said to "work." And in 1980, a team of psychologists, after summarizing the case studies of 475 clients undergoing talk therapy, overwhelmingly concluded psychotherapy to be efficacious. Putting aside the extraordinary difficulty involved in determining the effectiveness of psychotherapy, the one question that the study failed to answer was why it was that no matter which school of therapy, they all seemed to work equally well. Other studies designed to find the best course of treatment have often produced not only suspect but also absurd conclusions. Regardless of credentials, school of psychotherapy, or length of treatment, the results were comparable. All this becomes intelligible when we recognize that since everything is a possible cause, then everything is a possible "uncause."

This forces us to reconsider what we mean by "cause" as it relates to the production of a negative emotion. As you may have noticed, all our attempts at establishing a cause have invoked the past, a bottom-up way to explain the present. The problem with this approach is that even when investigating simpler non-human phenomena, it is much easier to reduce downward, than it is to explain upward. Typically, complex phenomena like emotions are reduced to initial (downward) forces, while failing to explain upward. That is because they do not take into account any end purpose. Using the familiar paradigm of the pitchfork prodding us from behind and the carrot luring us toward the future, all our attention thus far has been exclusively on the pitchfork. This retrospective approach is how virtually all scientists and non-scientists causally explain natural phenomena.

In scientific circles the teleological definition of cause, the carrot, as it were, has virtually disappeared. "Cause," in this sense, means goal-driven and translates into "for the purpose of." Although in physics there are such things as attractors, a set of physical properties towards which a system tends to evolve *regardless of the starting conditions,* the majority of scientists believe that nothing in chemistry, biology, physics, geology, astronomy, and cosmology has ever provided evidence for purpose in nature. Except for some biologists where life forms are seen as pursuing selective advantages (most would disavow "purpose" and replace it with "directionality") and a few intrepid neuroscientists and physicists who are not uncomfortable with the notion of purpose as it relates to natural events, most scientists look askance at such a purposive explanation, because it smacks of the supernatural, a relic of our prescientific past. Unfortunately, this prejudice tends to be carried over into trying to explain psychological phenomena as well. Whenever an explanation for behavior is sought, the focus is rarely on the carrot; i.e., the future. This is not to entirely dismiss the influence of the pitchfork, but if we have any hope of trying to account for negative emotions, an omission of the carrot would make that impossible.

As regards negative emotions, our metaphorical carrot, simply defined, is a state of negative anticipation. The following two dialogues will crystallize what I mean. Unlike the preceding case studies, whose focus was on real, environmental objects like people, things, and events in the past and the present, while paying negligible attention to the future, the following two dialogues pay scant attention to the past and present, and focus entirely on the future instead—the point being that regardless of what we focus on or the time frame within which they occur, fear of the future initiated by self-doubt is what always lies at the heart of a negative emotion.

## Hypochondria

Setting: Harold is fifty years old and a college professor. He is married to a loving wife and has a young daughter whom he adores. He is a frustrated novelist whose anxiety seems to grow with each passing year. He has a history of hypochondria.

Harold:         As long as I can remember, I have been acutely aware of the risk of contracting illnesses. Lately, it's gotten worse.

In the past, I've concentrated on the obvious symptoms implicated in lethal diseases like cancer and heart attacks, but now it's gotten so that virtually anything unusual that occurs in my body becomes an obsessive concern.

PS: What would you like me to help you accomplish?

Harold: To find out why I'm getting worse.

PS: Might it have something to do with the fact that you are getting older?

Harold: No doubt. For the obvious reason that, as we get older, we come closer to dying.

PS: The reason may not be as obvious as you think. In any case, why do you fear dying?

Harold: I will not have accomplished what I wanted. I will die never having fulfilled what I thought I might become.

PS: What is that?

Harold: A major novelist.

PS: If you were a major novelist, do you think your fear of dying would subside?

Harold: I think I would be less fearful. But I still think I would be afraid.

PS: Do you know what it means to be afraid?

Harold: I wouldn't be here if I didn't. Every time I have a headache, I suspect *brain tumor,* and I become paralyzed with fear. If my stools seem dark—*aha! colon cancer.* If I have a tingling in my fingers, I suspect transient ischemic attack and possible stroke. If I have a weak stream, prostate cancer. I've become a walking encyclopedia of medical symptomology. I subscribe to medical journals like the *New England Journal of Medicine, Lancet* and all kinds of newsletters. And I never miss an opportunity to learn about some new and possibly deadly disease. It doesn't matter what tests I take, they're all "false negatives." [Laughs]

PS: What I meant was, is there a way of reformulating what you mean when you say that you are afraid? You see, when

|          | someone says that he is fearful, it is one of those words that suggest the presence of something palpable, something real inside us. |
|----------|-----------------------------------------------------------------------|
| Harold:  | Well, isn't it?                                                        |
| PS:      | Actually, fear is a point of view, a belief that if such and such came to pass, you would not be able to handle it. |
| Harold:  | That sounds like what I'm feeling. But how is what you have just said an improvement over using the word "fear?" I'm not sure what it means to say that I couldn't handle something. |
| PS:      | That you would be unhappy.                                             |
| Harold:  | That would be understating it. It would feel more like panic.         |
| PS:      | All right, *very* unhappy. But do you see the value of seeing fear as a point of view, a belief about a future event that you believe would make you unhappy? |
| Harold:  | I'm not sure.                                                         |
| PS:      | I can make that clearer. Most people think of fear as something mysterious, an "it" largely beyond our control. But if fear is only a point of view, that can be changed. |
| Harold:  | You mean I'm choosing to fear death?                                  |
| PS:      | Yes. Do you believe that beliefs can be forced upon you against your will? |
| Harold:  | There is such a thing as brainwashing and conditioning.               |
| PS:      | Were you brainwashed or conditioned to fear death?                    |
| Harold:  | No, but the awareness of death is universal.                          |
| PS:      | Yes, but not everyone is as preoccupied with it as you are. And I'm not even referring to martyrs, heroes, and those who believe in the hereafter. |
| Harold:  | All right, I've chosen to fear death.                                 |
| PS:      | Are we agreed then that fear is a point of view, a belief?            |
| Harold:  | Yes, but how will knowing that really solve my problem?               |

PS:    Do you believe it is possible to hold a belief for which there is no redeeming value?

Harold:    Maybe I have an unconscious death wish.

PS:    If that sometimes appears plausible, it only happens when you become so hopeless that the prospect of dying appears to be a way out. *You* know that you want to live. You wouldn't be talking to me if that were not true.

Harold:    I do want to live, yes.

PS:    Then I repeat, what is the redeeming value of believing that you have to make yourself afraid of dying? It must be connected to living.

Harold:    You seem to suggest that it has to be. Can't fear be irrational, exist for no reason?

PS:    You may mean no *obvious* reason. But fear is never gratuitous. It may seem irrational, but it is never created without a reason.

Harold:    What is my reason for making myself afraid of dying? … It seems to me that I'm afraid of not being afraid. Is that called phobophobia?

PS:    No, that is fear of being afraid. You're afraid of *not* being afraid—what do you mean when you say that you are afraid of not being afraid?

Harold:    I don't know, maybe it's like that expression "a watched pot never boils." It's almost as if I focus on this or that symptom; I prevent it from happening. It's like a talisman. It gives me the power to prevent things from happening or getting worse. Disease always seems to sneak up on you. Cancer and heart attacks are notoriously silent killers. Anyway, I know it's magical thinking, but I must believe that this vigilance protects me.

PS:    Do you believe that you would be less vigilant if you didn't make yourself focus on various bodily symptoms?

Harold:    Put that way at this moment I don't.

PS:    Will that knowledge solve your problem?

Harold:    Not entirely.

PS :    If not entirely, it is either that you need more time to trust what you just learned or that there may be another reason.

Harold:    Maybe fear is an atavistic remnant of our reptilian brain—you know a sort of fight or flight reflex that overrides what we do in our head.

PS:    Even if that were true, that would only apply in situations where there was an immediate threat and would pass when there was no longer any immanent danger. You used the word "talisman," but talismanic thinking is symbolic thinking, which means that it does have to do with what you do in your head and not the spontaneous effect of some archaic brain vestige.

Harold:    Okay, then what may be the other reason that I still make myself afraid of dying?

PS:    There are two ways to approach your problem. We can change your belief as to why death is bad, in which case the whole justification for making yourself afraid as a way of protecting yourself against it would disappear. But let's defer that subject for now. Or we can try to convince you that making yourself afraid won't protect you from dying. Let's start with the less ambitious objective. What are you afraid would happen if you didn't make yourself afraid of dying? What is the reason?

Harold:    The first thing that comes to mind is that I would be arrogant.

PS:    To whom would you appear arrogant?

Harold:    This is sounding weirder as I think about it. It seems that I would incur the wrath of the gods.

PS:    And they would punish you for your lack of humility? What would they do to you?

Harold:    I guess, hasten my death.

PS:    I guess we discovered the other reason. Do you now believe that if you no longer made yourself afraid of dying that it would be perceived as arrogance, and you'd be punished for it?

| | |
|---|---|
| Harold: | No. |
| PS: | And while we are at it, let's revisit the other reason. Do you still believe that if you didn't meticulously scrutinize bodily feelings that you would be less vigilant and more likely to die? |
| Harold: | No, but I'll need some more time to think about that. |
| PS: | I expect you to. For the moment, however, I hope death has lost some of its sting. |

## Acrophobia

Setting: Alex is a New York City official who has been afraid of heights most of his adult life. So far, he has managed to hide this by maneuvering himself into sedentary, administrative positions. He has been offered advancement, but the new position requires greater locomotion and exposes him to situations involving heights. Recently, he has had several panic attacks driving over bridges.

| | |
|---|---|
| Alex: | Did you ever take the Verrazano? That damn bridge never ends! |
| PS: | It seems to have brought you here. |
| Alex: | People make all kinds of suggestions. Don't think about it. Don't look down. They say some fear of heights is normal. How do I get over it? |
| PS: | By finding out what's really behind the fear. |
| Alex: | I've been afraid of heights as long as I can remember. My earliest recollection was when I was a teenager. I remember standing on a terrace high up, maybe twenty floors, and I started to feel weak in the knees. It's been pretty much like that ever since. |
| PS: | Do you remember what you are thinking at the time? |
| Alex: | No. I don't seem to be thinking anything, except falling to my death. |
| PS: | Suppose I were a miracle worker, and I instantly relieved you of your phobia … would you have any objections? |

| | |
|---|---|
| Alex: | Of course not. The constant fear of death is debilitating. It is crippling my career and affecting my relationships. |
| PS: | If falling didn't lead to death, would you have any reason to be afraid of falling? |
| Alex: | But it *would* lead to death. I can't take the two ideas apart. |
| PS: | For the moment, let's treat them separately. Is there anything you might say about falling other than it is dangerous? |
| Alex: | If I remember right, didn't Freud say that fear of falling has to do with sex? |
| PS: | Yes, he did. What do you think he meant? |
| Alex: | I'm not a professional. I'm not sure. But I don't think he meant sexual in the genital sense. |
| PS: | Then in what sense do you think he meant it? |
| Alex: | I guess in some pleasurable sense. Something about letting go. |
| PS: | I think you're right. Falling can be very pleasurable, and it can also be very dangerous. |
| Alex: | I just remembered something when I was a little boy. I recall how I used to love the rides my father used to take me on at Coney Island. I know what you are thinking. |
| PS: | What am I thinking? |
| Alex: | That I must have had some bad experience, and that's why I am afraid of heights. I never did. Do you believe me? |
| PS: | I wasn't thinking that at all. |
| Alex: | But doesn't a bad experience when you're a kid lead to the kind of fear I have? |
| PS: | Not necessarily. What is the connection between your experience as a boy and your present fear of heights. |
| Alex: | When I was a kid, we'd play chicken. It was dangerous and fun. |

PS: And if you allowed yourself to think falling was dangerous and fun, what are you afraid would happen?

Alex: I would be unguarded, and I would fall.

PS: Because you might enjoy the prospect of falling like you did when you were a little boy?

Alex: Yes, that's why I keep myself afraid. Am I doing the same thing when I get panic attacks going over bridges?

PS: Yes, it's only a variation on a theme. You focus on losing control of the car or some structural defect in the bridge in order to make yourself afraid for the same reason.

Alex: That's exactly what I do. I know this may sound stupid, but I can't help feeling that maybe it works. I'm still here.

PS: What makes you believe that you wouldn't be just as safe if you didn't make yourself afraid of falling? I should think getting weak in the knees would be a liability that would put you in greater danger. What makes you think you're not still alive in spite of your fear and not because of it?

Alex: I think all this could be useful in no longer making myself afraid of falling, but we still haven't dealt with my fear of dying. After all, that is really the point of all my maneuvering. None of this helps me not be afraid of death.

PS: If fearing heights is what you do because you mistakenly believe it would make you more careful, then theoretically, at least, it might apply to anything you make yourself afraid of. Why do you make yourself afraid of death?

Alex: It can't be because it would make me more careful about dying.

PS: Why not?

Alex: It absolutely does not seem to be my experience.

PS: You said that before. Let's pursue the possibility that you are doing something similar. You may have noticed that making yourself afraid keeps you from living fully. It keeps you from being happy.

Alex:      Yes, I've done that most of my adult life. I'd be excited about planning a vacation. Then I think that there's sure to be some damn cable car. But I still don't see what that has to do with staying alive.

PS:      Let's look for the connection. There's something about being happy—even if you were to stop being afraid of heights and bridges, and cable cars. If you allowed yourself to be happy, what is there about that that scares you?

Alex:      I don't know. It isn't the same thing as making myself afraid of falling. It doesn't make me more careful, or anything like that.

PS:      All right, then it must be something else. There must be something about being happy that in your mind works against longevity. Think, what might that be?

Alex:      If I were happy, time would fly by. You know how when you're having a good time, it seems to go faster.

PS:      Is there anything about time going faster that you don't like?

Alex:      Life would go faster, and life would seem shorter. It would be over before you knew it.

PS:      I see. Being unhappy makes time seem to go slower, not chronologically, of course. You are referring to psychological time. You're prolonging your life by making yourself afraid of dying. In a sense it works. Subjectively, life does seem longer. The question is, do you want to live that way? Were you born to survive or to be happy? Survival only matters because it gives us time to be happy. Do you agree?

Alex:      Yes, I can see what I'm doing, but I've been doing it all my life. I don't know if it's really possible to change.

PS:      There's every reason to believe that you will. The big difference now is you have all the right questions and all the right answers. Think about what you are doing and why you have been doing it. You will see that everything will change.

| Alex: | You give me a lot to think about. Well, the Verrazano is still a very long bridge. |
|-------|------------------------------------------------------------------------------------|
| PS:   | I assure you that it will get shorter.                                             |

It should be emphasized that, in these dialogues, phobias are treated as beliefs, and *beliefs always involve the future*. It has long been recognized by psychotherapists that the inability to stay in the here and now underlies all negative emotional states. We either get caught up in the fearfully anticipated future or focus on the past, but even the past, as it turns out, only gets our attention because we are afraid it has implications for the future. It is that omnipresent "what if" kind of thinking that defines anxiety. Freud believed that anxiety was the core problem in the treatment of emotional disturbances. So, however we choose to view unhappiness—as distinctly named negative emotions or as different manifestations of anxiety—the crucial point in either case is that negative states are always anticipatory. "The worst is yet to come" is the concomitant belief that underlies all instances of unhappiness experienced in the present. Not being in the here and now always means that we are worried about what is going to happen next.

Homo sapiens reign supreme because the larger brain that endowed us with a long-range memory also endowed us with the capacity for long-range anticipation. It is a defining characteristic of human consciousness. It is what has enabled us to head off catastrophe better than all other animal species and magnified our numbers. It is not surprising that the insurance industry is the largest business enterprise in the world. We plan for illness, accidents, natural disasters, obsolescence, and loss. Usually, purchasing an insurance policy is one of the good ways to anticipate. Unfortunately, the ability to anticipate also enables us to dread. When we anticipate what can go wrong, and plan accordingly, it is one thing; but when we *worry* about such a possibility no matter what plans are possible or in place, that is entirely another. Anticipation and fear are not the same thing. Worry is a choice; it is not imposed on us by our environmental past.

Environmental psychologists would disagree. They believe that the environmental object is indeed the cause of fear. They believe that when treating phobics, the individual must be conditioned to disassociate the stimulus–response connection between the object and the fear. Avoidance, substitution, gradualism, and inundation are some of the techniques employed. In addition to *avoiding the object* of the phobia altogether, behavioral therapy may *try to substitut*e a less commonly encountered object. It might be a more manageable problem if, for example, the fear of dogs were replaced by a fear of zebras. *Gradualism* is another approach. With a partner who walks her through it, the phobic is gradually exposed to the anxiety-producing object. The agoraphobic is counseled to venture just onto her front porch, leaving her door open behind her; or to focus on the rewards of a destination, such as a walk to her mailbox, where a letter from her daughter may await her. A hydrophobic is assisted by a partner who gets the phobic to put one toe in the water, then the ankle, and so on. Another approach is *inundation,* where the phobic is completely immersed in the feared object. That's what literally happens when hydrophobics are thrown into a pool. The results, as with all such techniques, are mixed. Some hydrophobics learn to swim for their lives, while others simply sink. No one can account for the difference.

We can be grateful for any technique that alleviates human suffering, but I would propose that there is a better way to deal with fearful states of mind. Our focus should be entirely on the question of how and why we come to hold beliefs. *What we decide to believe is always guided by what we consider to be useful for getting what we want or avoiding what we don't.* And we can do that by mistakenly making ourselves afraid. We can literally make ourselves afraid of anything, even fear itself, and that is called phobophobia. There is really not much to learn from phobophobia, because it's not the fear of being afraid that presents a problem, but rather the fear of *not* being afraid: *If I didn't make myself afraid of* (fill in the blank)*, the very thing I don't want to happen is more likely to happen.* There is no word for this fear. I propose *aphobophobia,* fear of fearlessness.

Throughout, I have been making the point that self-doubt alone is the source of our unhappiness, but if fear is also always part of a negative emotion, isn't that assertion weakened? Not really. The fearful person is always asking, "Can I trust myself to avoid what I don't want, and can I trust myself not to get unhappy if I fail?" If we agree that fear is self-imposed and that it can only happen when a person does not trust him or herself to make the right choices, then it ought to be clear that fear and self-doubt can never be separated.

To be fair and in the interest of accuracy, the question that we should ask at this point is: *Can we be sure that there are there no exceptions?* Many would claim that not all our so-called negative emotions make us feel like passive victims riddled with self-doubt and fear. Jealousy, resentment, embarrassment, envy, depression, and a long list of other negative emotional states are, at their core, obviously self-deprecatory and anxiety-ridden; but what about emotions like anger and grief? It is not obvious that these emotions necessarily involve either fear or self-doubt. They may even appear respectable, if not praiseworthy. Anger often seems to be active, other-directed, vigorous, and productive, and grief, when it doesn't lead to depression, is a sadness that seems to qualify as the most human, compassionate, and commemorative of emotions. Let's see.

## Anger

Setting: Andrew owns a medium-size company. He is ambitious and a hard worker. He has been married to a gentle, soft-spoken woman for three years. He complains that she doesn't seem to listen to him when he talks to her. She, on the other hand, while seeming to agree that what he asks of her is not unreasonable, finds herself unwilling or unable to do what he wants. She told him that she doesn't know why, but she is not sure she loves him anymore.

| | |
|---|---|
| Andrew: | I think my marriage is falling apart, and I am hoping you can help me. |
| PS: | What is the problem? |
| Andrew: | I'm not sure. Nothing seems to get through to her. I'm married to an intelligent woman who seems to act like an idiot. She tunes me out. I have to tell her things over and over before anything registers, and even then she often forgets—or seems to. |
| PS: | You seem to be very angry. |
| Andrew: | Wouldn't you be? |
| PS: | What kinds of things do you tell her to do? |
| Andrew: | I don't want you to think that I don't consult her. I ask her, not tell her. |
| PS: | Give me an example. |
| Andrew: | Oh—it's a small thing, but it's typical. I love the perfume Shalimar. I've given it to her, but she never puts it on. I've asked her, and she says she just doesn't think of it. |
| PS: | Does she like Shalimar? |
| Andrew: | Yes, she says she does. I even asked her. |

115

| | |
|---|---|
| PS: | Do you believe her? |
| Andrew: | Why in God's name would she lie? |
| PS: | She might be afraid of you. |
| Andrew: | Good God. I don't come on like, "You'll wear the Shalimar or else!" I literally shower her with the sort of things women are supposed to want. I give her options. I say, "Tell me yes or no!" She's got everything. |
| PS: | On the surface, perhaps. |
| Andrew: | What do you mean? |
| PS: | Let me point out that virtually everything you've said to me so far has been in a state of anger. |
| Andrew: | Well, look what I've been putting up with! Anyway, I can't help my personality. I'm a very wired type. |
| PS: | Do you like being an angry man? |
| Andrew: | If you put it that way, it has its up and downsides. |
| PS: | What's up about it? |
| Andrew: | It's better than being depressed. You've go to admit that! |
| PS: | Do you tend to get depressed? |
| Andrew: | I fight it. Only a wimp lets himself get depressed anyway. |
| PS: | You still haven't told me why you're angry. You've only told me it beats depression. |
| Andrew: | How can you not get angry if you expect anything to get done? My workers wouldn't respect me if they weren't afraid of me. |
| PS: | So you use anger as a way of getting people to move. Does it always work? |
| Andrew: | With most of them. The other kind don't last long. |
| PS: | Does it work with your wife? |
| Andrew: | She sort of spaces out. It doesn't seem to matter whether it's, "This suit needs to go to the cleaners," or "Get packed; I've booked a cruise for the two of us!" And still, I tell you, she's no airhead! |

PS:      Then why do you continue to do it?

Andrew:      What else can I do, let it pass when she doesn't seem to hear me? If I did that with that people who work for me, I'd be out of business in a month.

PS:      But there is an enormous difference in your relationships to your employees and that with your wife.

Andrew:      Of course there is. My employees know my wife is absolutely number one. I think it's even a kind of joke with them.

PS:      But I don't think you have spelled it out.

Andrew:      What do you mean?

PS:      Do you care what your employees think of you?

Andrew:      It doesn't pay to bend over backwards to be popular with employees. To employees you're just the boss, and we can do business as long as they remember that. I keep it impersonal.

PS:      I think that is a bad management attitude. The best you can get with an angry management style is compliance, not loyalty. But let that go for the moment. In any case, that approach will only get the same results with your wife. You may have noticed that even when she does what you ask—even packs for a cruise—it isn't done with real enthusiasm.

Andrew:      I guess that's true. She just sort of goes along.

PS:      Is that what you bargained for when you got married? If you did, you're settling for very little. Permit me to tell you what I know that you really want from her:
You don't want her to do what you want. You want her to *want* to do what you want.

Andrew:      Yes, yes, that's exactly what I want. But how do I get it?

PS:      First, discredit your anger as a method of dealing with people generally, and with your wife in particular.

Andrew:      What do you mean by discrediting it? Do you mean not show my anger? Just grit my teeth?

PS:        No, that won't work. It is next to impossible to hide. It will always be reflected in your behavior. Besides, your wife knows your style. More important, anger is a painful state of affairs. For that reason, I should think you would want to stop being that way.

Andrew:    But the only thing that seems to help is when I let it out. Are you saying I should just bottle it up? Stew inside?

PS:        I don't mean that. All you are doing is letting off steam, and all that does is to release what is already there. For your information, there is debate going on among psychologists. There are those who maintain that ventilating anger is therapeutic, and those who claim that such an approach encourages people toward more and more anger.

Andrew:    What do you think?

PS:        They are both right and both wrong. For some people, that would be true and for others not. In any case, both schools are missing the point because they are only dealing with the expressive aspects of anger. To express or not to express, is *not* the question. Their mistake is that they both treat anger as a given. I'm interested in why anger occurs in the first place. If we can find *that* out and prevent it from happening, the question of expressing it or not becomes academic.

Andrew:    How do I not get angry?

PS:        Let's break it down. Would you agree that it appears to happen when something is not going your way? A traffic jam, an employee that doesn't seem to catch on fast enough, a wife who appears to be resisting your efforts, for example. You may have noticed even trivial events can trigger your anger.

Andrew:    Yes, it always starts with frustration.

PS:        It is the feeling that you are being stopped from getting what you want. And the object of your frustration always seems to be outside yourself—and that is the illusion. Let's grant that anger starts with the awareness that you're being prevented from getting what you want. But the anger is *what you do* with that awareness.

Andrew: What do I do? In, say, a traffic jam, sure I blow my horn, I curse. I don't jump out of my car and yell, "Hey, dick head," and punch the stalled driver.

PS: By virtue of the fact you have just pointed out, that not everyone responds the same way, you see that the explanation of your behavior must reside in you. Why is anger necessary?

Andrew: I told you, to get people to move. They're wasting my life!

PS: And we agreed that what you really want is for your wife to do what you want and to do it willingly. And we further agreed it succeeds in doing neither.

Andrew: I agree, but I don't think knowing all this is going to make a grain of difference in how I react.

PS: What does that tell you?

Andrew: I'm a stubborn bastard?

PS: It tells you that if you know that your anger is counterproductive and you still find it so hard to stop, that means that the anger is really directed at yourself for reasons we have not clarified.

Andrew: How do you figure that?

PS: You're the one who is experiencing the self-inflicted suffering. So it follows you must need it for reasons beyond getting others to move. Why do you need to be angry with yourself?

Andrew: [pause] I'm afraid not to be. If I weren't angry, I would be depressed. If I were depressed, I'd … disappear.

PS: You'd vanish from the face of the earth?

Andrew: I'd be nothing! I'd crawl into my shell, turn my face to the wall, and vegetate. I wouldn't be a force. At least now, they notice me. Of course, maybe mainly it's a case of like in that old line, "Not if I see you first." So they watch out for me. "Cool it, here he comes!"

PS: At any rate, anger directed at others is really anger directed at yourself. What you earlier called "your personality" is really an angry man who is afraid of disappearing, of being nothing. Andrew, could a man who is not angry also not disappear?

Andrew: I hope so. I'm tired of being angry.

PS: It is so. A man cannot aspire to be at peace with himself, if he really thought it was impossible.

Andrew: Are you saying that I can stop being angry and not lose who I am?

PS: Yes. You don't ever have to be angry in order to remain visible.

Andrew: And if I manage to believe that, it would settle my relationship with my wife and everyone else.

PS: Yes.

## Grief

Setting: Gale is a model whose career in the last year has become very successful. Her mother has been dead for two years and Gale finds that her grief over her death has not abated, and it seems to be getting worse.

Gale: I can't seem to get my mother's death out of my mind. I can't concentrate on my work. I have everything I could possibly want, and I spoil it all with my obsessive thoughts about my mother.

PS: Do you have any idea why this is happening?

Gale: I know it's normal to grieve over the death of people you love, but this is morbid. It has been two years.

PS: At what point does grief become morbid? Six months, a year, two years?

Gale: When you put it that way, it sounds arbitrary. There is no point.

PS: Then what you call morbid is what you decide is morbid.

Gale: It doesn't feel like I'm deciding anything.

PS: All right, if you don't like the word "decide," I'll put it another way. If periods of grief depend on each individual, they can only be explained on the basis of how each person views the event. How you view it is really a choice, although it may not seem like one at the time.

Gale: I think that for some people it takes more time to heal the sorrow than others.

PS: Why is that do you suppose? What do you think determines the amount of time that each person requires?

Gale: You're not going to tell me a decision, are you?

PS: Do you have a better theory?

Gale: No.

PS: Then bear with me. Suppose people do decide for themselves what constitutes a respectable period of mourning, and that at some point they just stop. I'm not suggesting that this is thought out ahead of time. Rather, the experience of sorrow seems to trail off with the passage of time. That leads to the conclusion that "time heals," which in turn suggests that time has some curative power, very much like what is required with a physical wound. But suppose this is all a mistaken analogy, which obscures the real psychological rationale for grief.

Gale: If that's true, I'd like to know what that is. [She sobs.] But I can't help myself; I loved her so. I miss her so.

PS: Would you ever want for your mother what she wouldn't want for herself?

Gale: Of course not.

PS: Would your mother want you to suffer the way you have been?

Gale: No. But the fact that she wouldn't makes me love her all the more. The knowledge that she would want me to be happy doesn't help; it just makes it worse.

PS: In any case, you're not giving her what she wants, which is for you to be happy. I only mention this to get you in touch with the fact that your grief doesn't benefit your

|        | mother, and so we must conclude that in some way it must be doing you some good. |
|--------|---------------------------------------------------------------------------------|
| Gale:  | According to that logic, there would be no point in holding a funeral, since it doesn't benefit the dead. |
| PS:    | But funerals are created to benefit the living. |
| Gale:  | I always thought they were held to show respect for the loved one. |
| PS:    | Yes, a public display to honor the memory of the deceased. People gather to openly demonstrate their respect for the departed. But for the last two years, you have continued to mourn with no notion of public bereavement, which is to say you have been engaging in a private wake. What are you trying to show yourself? |
| Gale:  | What am I trying to show myself? |
| PS:    | What would you say about a person who didn't grieve for her mother? |
| Gale:  | That she didn't love her. |
| PS:    | That is certainly not true of you. |
| Gale:  | No, it's not. |
| PS:    | Does it feel good to know that you love your mother? To put it another way, does it give you a good feeling to know that you are paying homage to your mother when you grieve? |
| Gale:  | Yes, but I'm finding all this a little confusing. |
| PS:    | We can clear it all up. Your original complaint was that you couldn't stop grieving. But you agree that grieving is your way of paying homage to your mother's memory. And you said that a person who doesn't grieve would not be a loving person. It follows that if you didn't grieve, you believe that you wouldn't be a loving person either. So grief is your way of being a loving daughter, and feeling like a loving daughter feels good. In effect, feeling bad enables you to feel good. |
| Gale:  | I follow your analysis, but that doesn't seem to fit my experience. |

PS:    That's because you are only accustomed to believing that your grief is caused by your mother's death, without also being aware that you regard it as necessary to prove that you're a loving daughter.

Gale:    I see what you're saying. But I do believe that if she were out of my mind, it would mean that she were out of my heart.

PS:    That dilemma is an illusion. Grief need not be a condition of love.

Gale:    I would like to be convinced.

PS:    I think you are very close to being convinced, but you may not be aware of it. I observe, for example, that you are much more relaxed than when you first walked into my office. Is that so?

Gale:    Yes, I am.

PS:    And does feeling more comfortable make you any less loving?

Gale:    I see what you mean. But another question, why did my grief seem to get worse when I started to become more successful?

PS:    That's easy. With success comes good feelings. Since you believed feeling good meant you'd become an unloving daughter, you had to fight all the harder to stay bereaved when the success came.

Gale:    Yes, my success would have allowed us to do many more things together. Now it's become a constant reminder that it will never happen. My mom and I always had this plan to go to Rome. She'd never been able to get to go anyplace, and she wasn't just your standard mother, you understand. She loved art; she was into things.

PS:    Whatever scenario you make up, its purpose will always be the same. You prevent yourself from being happy because you mistakenly believe you wouldn't be a loving daughter otherwise. It's a fiction you made up to prove that you are not bad.

# 10

# Fictions–Why We Make Things Up

*Virtue is not the reward of happiness but happiness itself.*
Benedict Spinoza

*The object of fear should be distinguished from the cause of fear, or delight in us (the object of fear, of delight) is not thereby its cause but—one might say—its focus.*
Ludwig Wittgenstein

For most people, the notion of fiction is suspect. We think anything made up is contrary to fact suggests fakery. While not dismissing that possible meaning, I am using the term in a more technical sense, as a linguistic invention whose usefulness in human affairs is indispensable. *Fictions* come in many varieties. They may be scientific, mathematical, religious, mythological, political; malefic or well intentioned. They are created to focus attention on a subject and to galvanize action. At its best, a fiction is *heuristic,* meaning that it stimulates interest for further investigation. That makes them crucial for learning and solving problems. On a serendipitous side note, it is notable that "heuristic" shares a paternity with the French word "heureux," which means happy.

Scientists and mathematicians necessarily employ *unobservable fictions.* For example, electromagnetism and gravity are immaterial fields that exercise force on material objects. Energy is a theoretical construct that cannot be seen or touched. Dark matter, the very large, and quarks, the very small, have never been observed. Physicists talk about subatomic particles, but these particles have neither solidity nor boundaries and are often referred to as *virtual* particles. A neutrino is a massless and spaceless particle. Scientific fictions are often testable and can lead to discoveries of measurable, natural events. For example, it was recently reported that a neutrino does contain some mass after all.

There is no sphere of problem solving that is more fictional than mathematics. How are we to understand things like *imaginary* numbers, such as the square root of minus one; that a straight line consists of a one-dimensional entity, bounded by two dimensionless entities called points; or an *asymptote* which is a line whose distance to a given curve tends to zero but never gets there. Mathematical fictions are essential to our understanding of physical phenomena, and pure mathematics is also heuristic in the way it leads to new knowledge and solves problems in computing, construction, population systems, and so on. And just as scientific fictions are testable, mathematical fictions are provable.

As we move away from the fictional world of the testable and the provable, we enter a fictional arena whose purposes are wholly different. We are all somewhat familiar with fictions, designed to get people to do and feel what their propagandists want them to. Demagogues could not function without them. The gods of the Aztecs demanded human sacrifice, and used Quetzalcoatl, the mythological feathered-serpent god, to justify that practice. Religious fictions like witches justified the Inquisition Political fictions such as liberty, justice, and equality—well intentioned or not—were the rallying cries for any number of bloody wars and countless human conflicts. Sometimes political fictions are masked with the aura of scientific respectability. Nazi scientists promulgated a genetic theory of the racial inferiority of "the Jew," which they used to create national solidarity and consolidate Hitler's power. At about the same time, Soviet Russia advanced an opposite theory, *Lysenkoism,* minimizing the significance of chromosomes and genes, because heredity collided with Bolshevist doctrine by implying that there were limits as to what could be changed by the state. Although vestiges of these points of view still survive, they are no longer regarded factually, nor are they any longer considered valid scientific hypotheses.

Pseudoscientific fictions are even more rampant in psychology. A whole lexicon of grandiloquent and vacuous jargon, what has often been disparaged as psychobabble, has littered the psychological landscape for the last fifty years. "Inner child," "meaningful relationships," "empowerment," "episodic dyscontrol," and a seemingly endless compilation of terminological gobbledygook try to persuade us that these fictions point to something factual and useful, when, in fact, they add little to our understanding of human unhappiness, nor do they solve any problems.

An earlier example of a pseudoscientific fiction masquerading as a fact, but in fact, pure propaganda, as it turned out, was the alleged evils of masturbation. Before masturbation was said to cause blindness, it was believed to cause insanity. It did neither. As a matter of record, masturbation, formerly classified as a disorder, is now even seen by a few professionals as therapeutic. The so-called harmfulness of masturbation had no medical or factual basis, nor was it useful as a fiction for generating new knowledge that would increase our understanding of either physical or psychological disorders. It would never be used to solve any problems because there was no problem to begin with. The fiction itself was the problem. It was a medical fiction posing as a fact, when, in reality, it was a veiled, moral proscription.

And this brings us to my central point. Although it is probably as old as the birth of language, the belief in human "imperfection" is also a pseudoscientific fiction with no factual basis. Now, if I am right that the belief that something is wrong with us is at the heart of all our negative emotions, we must now pause to reconsider what investigators are really asserting when they make statements about negative emotions. A little tutorial in elementary logic can help us out.

## The Fiction of Human Imperfection—a Logical Analysis

All statements can be divided into two kinds of propositions: empirical and analytic. Empirical propositions are those that have factual content; these refer to things other than themselves. Analytic propositions are self-definitional, which is to say they refer to nothing in the tangible world. Here are some examples of empirical statements from differing schools of thought:

- Jealousy is a gut reaction to territorial encroachment (visceral).
- Jealousy is an evolutionarily adaptive predisposition (genetic).
- Jealousy is the result of repeated rejection (environmental).
- Jealously is produced by a biochemical imbalance (psychopharmacological).

Notice that in each of these statements, the predicate—everything to the right of the subject, "jealousy"—links the emotion to the external or internal world of "facts." In other words, they claim the feeling is caused by real things in the sensible world.

On the other hand, emotional statements that are analytic are self-defining:

- Jealousy is the green-eyed monster.
- Jealousy is the only emotion that always occurs within the context of three people.

These statements are analytic because they are true by definition, i.e., devoid of factual content. True by definition means that the predicate is already contained in the subject. In the first instance, "green-eyed monster" is a Shakespearean poetic figure, which is now interchangeably identified with the emotion. In the second instance "the only emotion that always occurs within the context of three people" (the third person may be real or imagined) is already implied by the subject "jealousy." In either instance, the only information these statements impart is that what appears to the right of the subject is transposable to what appears to the left. They simply redefine themselves in equivalent terms in the same way that we can say that bachelors are unmarried males or 2 + 2 = 4. They are equations.

Although symbolic logic and mathematics may use different notations, they both live in a world of self-definitional abstractions. Henri Poincare, the great French mathematician, called mathematics the art of finding the same name for different things. That is why the truth of mathematics and logic is referred to as *empty* or tautological; they do not say anything about the sensible world. Consistent with this analysis, let us see if investigators studying emotions are engaging in a similar activity.

Consider the following syllogisms:[7]

## General Emotion

| If | The belief that one is bad causes one to feel bad. |
| --- | --- |
| And | To feel bad is to believe that one *is* bad. |
| Then | The belief that one is bad causes the belief that one is bad. |

---

7    A syllogism is a three- step exercise in deductive reasoning.

## Specific Emotion

| If | The belief that one is bad causes one to feel jealous. |
|---|---|
| And | To feel jealous is to believe one is bad. |
| Then | The belief that one is bad (jealous) causes the belief that one is bad (jealous). |

As we can see, the conclusions in both instances are circular. They don't even qualify as definitions, because the subject is reproduced verbatim in the predicate. This means that emotional statements are as self-defining as those of mathematics or logic. The only information such statements convey is that what appears to the right of the subject is transposable with what appears to the left; it simply redefines itself in the same way that bachelors are unmarried males or 2 + 2 = 4. Consequently, it would be as senseless to say that believing that one is bad causes a bad feeling or to believe that one is bad causes jealousy as it would be to say that two plus two causes four. Thus, we can say, in the manner of Poincare, that psychology has been engaging in the mistaken art of finding different names for the same thing.

Psychological statements—at least those that express negative emotional states—are empty, merely definitional. We are merely substituting one term for another by a process of definition. And since definitions exist because we choose to use a term in a particular way, it would be incoherent to ask if it were true. It would be tantamount to asking if a decision is true.

Now, if the decision to believe that we are bad is equivalent to saying we feel bad, the mind–body question need not bewilder us anymore. We have always known that in actual linguistic practice, there has always been a close association between statements that begin with "I believe" and "I feel." In the context of negative self-reference, the association between them is not only semantic; it is experiential. You cannot believe that you are stupid and not feel stupid, that you are ugly and not feel ugly, that you are bad and not feel bad. In sum, an emotion does not comprise two near-simultaneous events, but rather it is a unified, solitary occurrence as instantaneous and indivisible as electricity, as unsequenced as a decision.

Spinoza, one of the important philosophers writing about emotions, said, "Virtue is not the reward of happiness but happiness itself." He was right because, psychologically speaking, to be virtuous is to believe one is good, and in terms of the present analysis, the absence of virtue is to believe that one is bad, which is unhappiness itself. Even if it were argued that what we think in our head and what we feel in our body are not instantaneous but, rather, two near-simultaneous events, there would not be any practical disadvantage. It only matters that all negative feeling states are reducible to the belief that we are bad. The mind–body relationship is one of identity and might be best depicted by the following diagram:[8]

Early on in the book, I stated that in order to understand negative emotions, the sequence of three elements had to be explained: the event–what takes place in the environment, and what takes place in our head and our body. We now know that what we do in our heads is equivalent to what we feel in our bodies, and we also know that nothing *causes* to us to believe that we are bad. Then what is the relationship between the environmental event and our emotions?

Wittgenstein observed, "The object of fear should be distinguished from the cause of fear, or delight in us (the object of fear, of delight) is not thereby its cause but, one might say, its focus." What is left out of that off-the-cuff observation is the normal mindset of those who are doing the focusing and the purpose of the focus. What I am referring to, of course, is the universally held belief that we are flawed. This normal frame of reference focuses on the limitless world of possible events and enables us to experience the entire range of nameable emotions. That relationship can be expressed in a formula or equation. Using the case studies cited throughout the book here are some examples:

---

8    It is worth noting that E. Jacobsen, after carefully conducted laboratory experiments, was unable to detect any time-lag between an electric stimulus and the experience of a subjective feeling.

## Belief that one is bad + focus = nameable emotion

# External Events

- Belief that one is bad + other woman = Jealousy
- Belief that one is bad + successful other = Envy
- Belief that one is bad + uncooperative wife = Anger
- Belief that one is bad + incestuous father = Resentment
- Belief that one is bad + solicitous other = Embarrassment
- Belief that one is bad + deceased parent = Grief (exogenous depression)
- Belief that one is bad + heights = Anxiety (Acrophobia)

# Internal Events

- Belief that one is bad + hormones = Depression (endogenous depression)
- Belief that one is bad + bodily symptoms = Anxiety (hypochondria)

# Objectless Events

- Belief that one is bad + meaninglessness = Depression (ennui)
- Belief that one is bad + open spaces = Anxiety (agoraphobia)

Of course, any classification of discrete emotions might be seen as somewhat arbitrary in that it tends to neglect the dynamic nature of our conscious life. Emotions, as we know, can combine and replace each other with such fluidity that it is difficult to know when one leaves off and another begins. By merely shifting our focus, we can evince another nameable emotion. Using our first example, when focusing on the other woman, we produce jealousy, focusing on what other people might think, we produce humiliation, focusing on one's unfaithful spouse, we produce anger, and so on.

Needless to say, the list does not exhaust the total inventory of nameable emotions. The number of negative experiences would comprise a very long list indeed. Many of the nameable negative emotions are virtually interchangeable. Except for their intensity, there is a strong family resemblance among the continuum of emotions variously labeled humiliation, shame, embarrassment, self-consciousness, and shyness. Similarly, rage, hatred, hostility, anger, resentment, irritation, and annoyance exist on a continuum. The same might be said for depressive states like dejection, sadness, melancholy, and burnout. Note that not even the focus on a tangible object is necessary for these negative states to take place. Objectless emotions like despair and forlornness, dominant themes of the existentialists, and psychoanalytic terms like anhedonia[9] and algolagnia,[10] I would suggest, are only veiled synonyms for depression and anxiety.

In any case, it should be noted that both depression and anxiety have been classified under three foci—external, internal, and objectless events. And similarly, grief is classified as reactive depression because it is believed to be caused externally, by the death of a loved one; endogenous depression is thought to be internally caused by a biochemical imbalance; and ennui, an objectless form of depression, is attributed to issues of meaninglessness. Although angst would be a classic example of objectless anxiety, I felt it so overlapped with ennui that any separate treatment would be redundant. So in our final dialogue, we'll look at a closely related state of objectless anxiety—agoraphobia. Although agoraphobia is not objectless in the strictest sense, its object is so free-floating and amorphous, it might as well be.

But for now let's consider the case of Eric:

## Depression

Setting: Eric is fifty-five years old. He is vice president of data processing for a multinational reinsurance company, which entails frequent trips to London, Rio, and Tokyo. Following a kidney stone episode about a year before, he gave up drinking, and more recently, smoking. He has a congenial marriage, and his two children—the younger still a student— are doing well. Recently, somber events have occurred within his circle: a colleague six years younger died of a heart attack, and his sister-in-law underwent a lumpectomy. Though widely respected in his field, he regards his expertise as "very limited." He dreads business travel, yet finds homecoming a letdown. He calls his family "close, as families go,"

---

9   Anhedonia is a condition marked by an inability to take pleasure in anything.

10  Algolagnia is a chronic state of displeasure wherein the complainer is disinterested in everything save his desire to prove how bad the future will be.

but describes a "Mother's Day celebration when the four of them went out to dinner as "deadly." He dabbles in philosophy. Eric came for an appointment following a night in which he wakened with chest pains. He told me, "I thought, *I'm going the way of poor Jerry* [the late colleague]. When I realized it was a just a cramp from the position I was lying in, it was almost a disappointment."

| | |
|---|---|
| Eric: | I don't want to waste your time and mine. Frankly, I'm not too optimistic about the outcome of this meeting. I've undergone long periods of psychotherapy, tried other therapeutic approaches, and I am pretty well read in philosophy, psychology, and religion. The results, as you can see, still leave my problem unresolved. Of late, I've become convinced that the only solution to my problem lies in religion. Frankly, I'm not very hopeful. |
| PS: | But with no hope at all, you wouldn't be here. |
| Eric: | It's true, I do harbor a kind of secret hope, or maybe it's nostalgia. I feel that I might regain a sense of meaningfulness through religion. But, there's no recapturing one's early faith. |
| PS: | You have at least partly regained your faith by recognizing the need for it. Have you ever read Pascal? |
| Eric: | "If only God would show His hand a little more, or a little less." How does it go? |
| PS: | How about, "Those who look for God have already found Him." |
| Eric: | One of my favorites! If only he were right. |
| PS: | If you didn't think he might be, would it be one of your favorite quotes? |
| Eric: | But why do I still have doubts? |
| PS: | You treat doubts as if they were necessarily bad. Have you ever considered that doubts might be opportunities to confirm what you wish were true? |
| Eric: | A little Pollyanna for me. |
| PS: | How about "Faith is the substance of things hoped for, the evidence of things yet not seen"—too Pollyanna? |

| Eric: | No. But ever since I grew up, I've been a skeptic. How can I suddenly accept a belief simply on the basis that I want to believe it? |
|---|---|
| PS: | By disabusing yourself of the idea that because you want something to be so, it's necessarily suspect. |
| Eric: | My god, it sounds like you're advocating a methodological approach that uses wish fulfillment as the way of arriving at truth. |
| PS: | Why not? I'm not encouraging you to distort or ignore objective reality. We are talking about what you personally want to believe as true. |
| Eric: | Even personal belief must be based on evidence. |
| PS: | Not really. Personal belief rests on what you are willing to accept as evidence. What constitutes evidence even among those who prize it the most is still an open question. The origin of life, the universe, or consciousness will never be settled by recourse to evidence. How ever well schooled we become in these matters, our philosophy of life will always be an act of faith. In any case, you're acting as if you have something to lose if you decided to believe in God. |
| Eric: | That sounds like Pascal's Wager, that it's safer to gamble on the idea that God exists, because giving up a lifetime of pleasure is worth avoiding a possible eternity of hell. |
| PS: | No, I'm saying that there is *no* wager. First, because loving God need not be an act of renunciation of the world. Second, if it turns out God exists after you're dead, you will have been proven right, and not only would you have had a happy mortal existence, you will share an eternity of happiness with God. But you can't be proved wrong, since it could only be proved to someone who survived his own death. In that case, you will have had a happy life loving God. There is no wager; either way you win. |
| Eric: | But I'm not any closer to believing in God. |
| PS: | Calculating odds as a way of getting to God is probably not the best way. I only tried to show you that argument and evidence would not convince anyone of the reality of |

God. If you find it hard to accept God, the explanation must lie elsewhere.

Eric:    I hope you're not going to serve up a rehashed distinction between what we can know in our heads and what we can know in our hearts.

PS:    I hope it's not a rehash. In any case, can we agree that if God is to have any meaning, it has to be a personal, loving relationship with him, which is to say that it would include what we do in our heads *and* what we feel in our hearts?

Eric:    Yes, but I still have to believe in him, in order to love him.

PS:    Are you familiar with the old medieval debate between Anselm and Abelard: *Does one believe in order to understand, or does one understand in order to believe?*

Eric:    Yes, that opens up a can of worms. I tend to go with Abelard. I presume you side with Anselm. I wish I could.

PS:    Maybe you can. We have been using several terms— "belief," "explanation," "truth," "evidence"—in a fairly haphazard way, but I think you might agree that they ultimately deal with the question *How do we know what we know?* The word "science" means knowledge. I think the confusion is that you are insisting that all knowledge must satisfy the criteria of scientific *method*. I might mention that even philosophers of science are not in agreement as to what that is.

Eric:    Whatever it is, scientific method wasn't merely invented. It's the distilled experience of the best brains throughout history. It is the measure against which knowledge must be judged.

PS:    To begin with, there are all sorts of unsettled issues as to what counts as scientific method. But even if there were unanimity, some of the most brilliant scientific brains—Copernicus, Kepler, Galileo, Pascal, Newton, and Einstein, arguably the finest scientific brains of their respective centuries—were not married to the scientific method as the only guide as to what they chose to personally believe. Copernicus, Kepler, and Galileo remained believing Christians all their lives; Pascal converted to Catholicism; Newton was an ardent theist who wrote more about religion than he did about science; and Einstein, albeit not in any orthodox sense, believed in the transcendent, referring to God as "the old one." You're familiar with his often-quoted remark, "Religion without science is blind, and science without religion is lame." None of these beliefs were arrived at using the scientific method, nor did any of them pay the slightest attention to what others thought.

Eric:     All right, subjecting all personal beliefs to the criteria of scientific acceptability may be a mistake. But why they believed what they did is still the question.

PS:      Without being flippant, the answer to that question is because it pleased them.

Eric:     Are you saying I can believe whatever I want?

PS:      Yes. Your present ignorance is something you unwittingly created by denying that.

Eric:     I would like to believe that, but I seem to be fighting that idea.

PS:      What are you afraid it would mean if you didn't?

Eric:     I would be simple minded, no better than a child. It just occurred to me that the closest I've ever come to having that relationship with God is when I was a boy. The idea of God being a loving father seemed to make everything make sense. And that's what I can't recapture.

PS:      Perhaps we might explore the nature of the father–child relationship from the other side. What did you like most about being a father yourself?

Eric:     It was similar to when my parents held me, only better. It was more peaceful, like when I believed in God when I was a boy.

PS:      But was it meaningful?

Eric: The word doesn't seem to apply.

PS: I was hoping you wouldn't think so.

Eric: Why?

PS: Because I wanted to point out that when you are happy, questions of meaningfulness are superfluous. Love answers all questions, because when you love, you feel what you want to feel. If a great authority tried to convince you that what you were feeling was an illusion, that your belief that you were loving your child was bogus, would he have any chance of succeeding?

Eric: Of course not.

PS: How can you be certain that you know that?

Eric: It feels true.

PS: Does love feel true because you believe it to be true, or do you believe it is true because it feels true? Which came first?

Eric: A variation on the debate between Anselm and Abelard.

PS: Or if we had to hone the question even finer. Is love, which feels true because it is consistent with what you want, the cause of faith in God; or is faith in God, which is also consistent with what you want, the cause of love?

Eric: Love is something that just happens. I'm not aware of ever having wanted anything. When you ask me if I want it to be true, it would seem to be consistent with what I want, but I can't be sure that wanting to have a loving relationship enabled me to have it.

PS: Let's see what we *can* be sure of. What we can say with certainty is that your belief that you feel love for your children is absolutely in accordance with what you want. It would hardly matter if you weren't aware of your wanting love in the beginning, or if it were a gift that fell into your lap. You didn't put any obstacles in the way of accepting it. All that mattered was that you let it happen.

Eric: Belief in God seems different. Maybe wanting to believe in God is the problem. I never consciously wanted to love my children. So maybe Pascal was wrong. Maybe those who look for God have not already found him, precisely because they're looking for him.

PS: It's not the wanting that is the problem; it's the way you look for God that prevents you from finding him. You have always insisted that faith in God had to precede your loving him.

Eric: That seems to be the way.

PS: Yes, but not the only way. Love may also precede faith.

Eric: How can love lead to faith?

PS: The closest you have ever come to loving God was when you were a little boy and when you were loving your own children. Why should that be?

Eric: Odd. I just remembered that St. Paul said something to the effect that when he became a man, he put away childish things.

PS: Ironically, what he meant by childish things were those things *not* having to do with the spiritual life and God. You drew the opposite meaning.

Eric: I guess childish things for me meant not wanting to be childish.

PS: I think you were conflating innocence with naïveté. Jesus said, "I assure you whoever does not accept the reign of God like a little child shall not take part in it." He knew that a child could love purely, because he has no false pride, no criteria of meaningfulness to satisfy. A child is good, and because of that, he loves without placing obstacles between himself and God.

Eric: Then I must have some notion that I am not good.

PS: What bad thing are you afraid you would discover about yourself if you gave yourself to God unconditionally?

Eric: I'm afraid I would be something of a simpleton. You know, we got a letter from my father-in-law. (My mother-in-law died a few months ago.) He had always been an agnostic. But he wrote, "I talk to God all the time. I find that God really does answer prayer." My son read it, and said, "Say, has Grandpa lost his marbles?" You know, that's the attitude everybody takes. Even my wife, Jan … she's a most understanding person, but she said to me, "You've given up drinking and smoking, and now you're looking for another crutch?" That's the attitude—second childhood.

PS: Would it be second childhood? It's an irony that the one thing that would allow you to have faith in God is the very thing you've been resisting. Is there anything about childishness that still troubles you now? Do you think it is a state of simple-mindedness?

Eric: I would like to think it is a state of humility. There is great truth in humility. Now that I think of it, I always felt closest to God in that state. It feels very much like it did when I used to pray as a boy.

PS: It's impossible to pray and not be childlike at the same time. I think that's what Jesus had in mind when he said, "I give you my word, if you are ready to believe that you will receive whatever you ask for in prayer, it shall be given to you."

Eric: And the way to become "ready to believe" is to be childish—what I was afraid of.

PS: And that's how "you will receive whatever you want if you ask it in prayer." Continue to believe that, and your depression will leave you.

## Anxiety

Setting: Anna is an architect. She is twenty-nine and has been married for two years. She has a history of phobias, starting with her going away to college. Shortly after getting married, she started to experience a generalized sense of anxiety, which subsequently developed into full-blown agoraphobia.

Anna: Would you mind if we left the office door ajar? I'd feel more comfortable if I could check to see that my mother is still in the anteroom.

| | |
|---|---|
| PS: | You have some reason to believe that she would leave? |
| Anna: | No. I just never go anywhere without her or my husband. |
| PS: | Why is that? |
| Anna: | I can't stand being by myself. |
| PS: | What would happen if you were by yourself? |
| Anna: | I might go crazy. |
| PS: | Is that possible? |
| Anna: | How do you mean? |
| PS: | If you really went crazy, how would you know it since you would be crazy? Besides, what makes you think that crazy people don't know what they're doing, that there isn't method to their madness? |
| Anna: | Are you saying that it's something that I'm making up? |
| PS: | It's worth considering. For example, you're feeling pretty crazy now. I would guess that somehow you must be aware of the fact that whatever else is going on, you must have some sense that you have something to do with it. |
| Anna: | I guess that's true. |
| PS: | But that's a secondary issue. Fear of going crazy came after you became afraid of being alone. |
| Anna: | But that is what is so confusing. Even as I tell you that I'm afraid of being alone, I'm also afraid of being with people. Public places terrify me. In fact, I always have to be seated next to the ladies' room. Just in case I have to get away. |
| PS: | From what? |
| Anna: | In case I get nauseous and throw up. |
| PS: | You're afraid that you might not be able to get to the ladies' room in time? |
| Anna: | Yes. I'd make a spectacle of myself. I'd be mortified. Wouldn't you be? |
| PS: | I can think of a lot of other things I'd prefer to have happen, but I wouldn't be mortified. |

Anna:     How could you not be?

PS:       By recognizing that vomiting is a natural function that can occur under any circumstances. Accidents are part of the human condition.

Anna:     But people are supposed to have control, be responsible.

PS:       Why do you believe that?

Anna:     And my husband would be just humiliated if I threw up in public.

PS:       Is what you fear, the humiliation of your husband?

Anna:     Yes. That would be the last straw.

PS:       What would he do?

Anna:     Leave. I couldn't make it alone.

PS:       Why do you believe that you couldn't manage alone?

Anna:     There'd just be a total void. I'd have nowhere to turn.

PS:       It seems to me that if you could come to believe that you would be all right alone, then the fear of throwing up in public would be less fearful, because even if it led to your husband's departure, you could handle it. That would go a long way in eliminating your agoraphobia.

Anna:     That's a very big if.

PS:       Nevertheless, would you love to believe that you would be okay if he did leave you?

Anna:     Yes, I would.

PS:       Suppose I told you I had the power to get you to feel okay if your husband left you, and that I could do that right now. Would you be totally receptive to it?

Anna:     I think so.

PS:       You hesitate. What does that tell you?

Anna:     That I may not believe you can do it. So I would be setting myself up for a disappointment.

PS:       But suppose you did believe I could do it, and you still hesitated. What would that mean?

Anna:     That I'm afraid of something.

| | |
|---|---|
| PS: | Exactly. What are you afraid it would mean if you allowed yourself to know that you could be okay without him? |
| Anna: | That I would no longer need him. |
| PS: | Would it *have* to mean you would no longer need him if you knew you would be okay without him? |
| Anna: | It wouldn't *have* to mean that, but to my husband it would. |
| PS: | Why do you say that? |
| Anna: | Because every time I start to feel better, he seems to act glum. Ever since we got married, he's always put constraints on me. Even when I *started* to have this problem and wanted to come for therapy, he absolutely refused. He said, "How can you buy that crap?" Now for some reason he's changed his mind and wants me to do therapy. He said, "Anything's worth a try. You can't go on like this." It's a total contradiction. |
| PS: | It only seems that way. There are no contradictions. Before you came to see me, what happened to change his mind? |
| Anna: | I was in the hospital for three weeks, because I was getting dizzy spells; I felt faint; I had trouble breathing, I even had tachycardia—you know, irregular heart beats. They found nothing physically wrong with me. A psychiatrist told me that they were "conversion symptoms." Anyway, I couldn't function, so my husband suddenly went along with my getting psychotherapy. |
| PS: | Tell me what your intuition is. If you were completely cured of your phobias, how do you think your husband would react? |
| Anna: | I think he'd be lost, quite frankly. |
| PS: | You're right. |
| Anna: | But then why is he telling me to do therapy? Does he want me to get well, or does he want me phobic? |
| PS: | He wants both. |
| Anna: | I don't get it. |

PS:        He wants you to believe that you are not okay without him, but he also does not want you to become a vegetable. That is why he encouraged you to do therapy when you were languishing in the hospital, and why he will try to discourage you if and when you start to come around. He wants you enfeebled, not destroyed.

Anna:     I don't believe he's as bad as all that.

PS:        Not bad, only insecure. But no more so than you.

Anna:     But I always thought of myself as a competent self-assured person.

PS:        So did he. And you were both correct. Can you figure out why you became no longer self-assured?

Anna:     Are you suggesting that if I were competent and self-reliant again, that I would be afraid he'd leave me?

PS:        I'm not suggesting that. You're only answering my question. But that is exactly why you became agoraphobic. You see, if you acknowledge the strategic purpose of acting as if you cannot be alone in order to ensure your husband does not leave you, you can no longer create a justification for not being self-reliant. You would, in effect, become a person who regained control of her life. And that is the solution to your anxiety. Let me remind you, anxiety, panic—what you will—always come from the feeling of being out of control.

Anna:     I think this all started way back before I even met my husband. In fact, it started after I went to college.

PS:        You were homesick?

Anna:     No. Everybody was so careful we shouldn't be. Weirdly enough, college was super-protective. My roommates made me the baby. They even called me "Bebe." One roommate was particularly super-maternal. She'd say, "I'm not going without my roomie." We'd have little tiny crushes on each other, not really, but like practicing for the main event

PS:        All that proves is that agoraphobia started with you. The people in your life are, at best, catalysts. You would likely have become agoraphobic even if your husband had no hidden agenda. You had already decided on your method of holding onto people.

Anna:     But how do I change?

PS:       Since we know that your mother has no vested interest in your being infirmed, let's start with her. If you allowed yourself to function autonomously, what would be the consequences in terms of your relationship with her?

Anna:     She'd be happy, and she wouldn't need to be always at my beck and call.

PS:       What might happen on the down side?

Anna:     When she saw that I could function independently, she wouldn't see me as much.

PS:       Even if you didn't see each other as much, wouldn't your being a competent person take a lot of strain out of the relationship? Wouldn't your mother feel grateful for your recovery and even get closer to you?

Anna:     Yes, and she'd get to brag to her friends how terrific I am. But that wouldn't be true of my husband.

PS:       Yes, at the outset he will even become more threatened. But if change is at all possible for him, it can only occur in that way. One thing is certain, however, the only way you are going to rid yourself of your phobia is to understand that it will never serve as the psychological glue that will keep your relationships together. Would you like me to close the door now?

Anna:     Yes.

# 11

# The Unified Theory of Unhappiness

*Happiness is no cultural value.*

Sigmund Freud

*This need for punishment is the worst enemy of our therapeutic efforts.*

Sigmund Freud

*Nothing is funnier than unhappiness.*

Samuel Beckett

*Love God and do as you please.*

St. Augustine

*The good man does not argue; he who argues is not good.*

Lao Tsu

*I give nothing as duties. What others give as duties, I give as living impulses.*

Walt Whitman

What remains to be done to complete our understanding of negative emotions is to find out why we might still resist believing that nothing is wrong with us. If this disquisition hasn't completely vaporized the notion that there is something wrong with us—of human imperfection, the reason is that there is still another dimension of human imperfection that needs to be addressed. So far, we have focused only on fallibility, which is unintentional and benign. We need also consider the possibility of the intentional and the malign in human nature. And although the possible existence of genetic evil was touched upon and repudiated in an earlier chapter, more needs to be said about our alleged cupidity. Except for those who believe that human beings are innately good and are made bad by society, the consensus is that people do bad things because they are naturally bad, and have to be constrained by society. Even strange bedfellows like materialists and moralists agree, with somewhat different agendas, that nature is, in Tennyson's phrase, "red in tooth and claw," and since we are part of nature, we are assumed to be similarly rapacious. Freud's entire system of thought, like most of the world's profound thinkers, rests on this alleged biological substrate. Freud refers to it, using his vivid metaphor, as "the seething caldron of the id."

My guess is that the acculturation aimed at taming our alleged malevolence probably began with the emergence of "taboo," which antedates belief in God, religion, and ethics. Because of its primordial canon of the forbidden, the unclean, and the profane, taboo's restrictive power remains operative in each of those subsequent systems of belief. Taboo serves as a template for how people ought to behave, and all underlying cultural conceptions of self are judged accordingly.

## Taboo, the Id, and Unhappiness

Observance of taboo is the universal rite of passage for anyone who wants to be a member of society. In order to ensure compliance, all advanced societies inculcate guilt. You may have noticed that guilt has been conspicuously absent among the emotions discussed so far. The reason for this is that guilt is not an emotion among equals. It is the seminal emotion that lies at the heart of all our unhappiness. But what is guilt other than a different name for what I have been calling the belief that we are bad—only more virulent because it carries with it the belief that we are the cause of other people's unhappiness. Now if it is true that the only source of our unhappiness is each person's belief that they are bad, then in what sense can it be said that we are guilty? Understanding this would make a "guilt trip" impossible because how can anyone make someone feel bad who didn't believe that they were bad? But since most of humanity remains unconvinced that we are not defective, this ubiquitously held belief in human rapacity in both religious and secular circles became the basis of morality and ethics and led to the inculcation of guilt because is still seen as the great civilizer and most efficient way restraining our alleged incivility.

Some of the best-known protagonists of Western culture who dared to put themselves beyond taboo suffered the gravest penalties for their presumption. Oedipus lost his eyes because of his hubris. Adam and Eve's loss of paradise was due to eating the fruit of knowledge of good and evil and placing themselves beyond God's command. Lucifer, "God's favorite," was condemned to hell for his pride. Not surprisingly, pride is ranked first among the cardinal sins. The subtext in all these narratives is clear—yield to authority … or else.

It follows that all advanced cultures extol virtues such as modesty, conformity, and deference to authority. They are behaviors that will be rewarded in this world or the next, while pride, hubris, and arrogance are swiftly and surely punished—not necessarily because such sins place the sinner outside of God's law, but because they place him outside of man's authority. Little wonder that genuflection and bowing are demanded in nearly all cultures. Walking tall is often a perilous game. This is not to say that acquiescing to authority is always to be avoided. Yielding to an authority that represents a spiritual or social, collective good may be a highly desirable human trait. There is a huge difference between yielding to authority because we agree with what it represents and doing so because we fear reprisal. So, at the end of the day, an authority is only an authority *on our authority*.

Needless to say, there are those who oppose deference to any and all authority. "Blessed are the meek for they shall inherit the earth" is the sort of self-effacing dictum that led critics like Nietzsche to revile Western morality as a slave doctrine.[11] I don't think he ever considered the possibility that *meekness* might be the experience of inborn egolessness, unpolluted by self-doubt. In any case, all his criticism did was to replace the religious view of imperfection with a secular one. When he says, "Man is unfinished and must be surpassed and completed," he merely offers another program for self-improvement, falling into the same error that all improvers of human nature fall into. They assume imperfection as a given, without recognizing that in so doing they have created an insoluble paradox. Let me remind you that "imperfection" is not a fact; it is a judgment of human beings—something we made up to fix what is assumed to be wrong with

---

11    My own view of this Christian beatitude is that its intention need not be understood as a moral imperative. It need not be a self-effacing prescription for becoming good, but rather a description of human beings who didn't believe that they were bad. Meekness, in this context, would simply designate the absence of self-deprecation. Accordingly, pride would disappear because it was an emotion that only came into being to compensate for what people thought was defective in the first place.

us. It is a negative self-referential fiction (the Liar's Paradox) which cannot be solved, only dissolved.

When we fail to recognize this, self-doubt filters our perceptions and predisposes us to see the world in the same way. It is this interplay between the belief that we are flawed and the world as it actually exists that leads us to conclude that there is something wrong with the world.. Then, we unwittingly fob off this projection as representing the "real world." In point of fact, *the real world* is at best mute, the clay of invention, communion, and industry, and at it's worst, lethal. The world can kill us, but it can't make us unhappy, at least not without our consent.

## The Pursuit of the Good

And that brings us to the most important question of all. *Why do we give consent?* If believing we are bad is equivalent to making ourselves unhappy, and we understand that this paradox is the cornerstone of our entire belief system, that it contaminates all our beliefs with a sort of madness, which includes the very rules by which we reason, why do we do that? How does one reason oneself out of madness? The way out is to realize that even in madness there is method, meaning that it is impossible to hold any belief, including a maddening one, unless it is seen to have redeeming value. The fact that all human endeavors necessarily seek what is good has not gone unnoticed throughout history. Although the implications were never fully worked out, Aristotle understood that "all knowledge and every pursuit aim at some good"; Thomas Aquinas held that "nothing is ever chosen except under its good aspect." Modern equivalents can be found in psychology and psychiatry. Abraham Maslow said that "neurosis is therapy" and R. D. Laing asserted that psychosis is "a special strategy invented in order to live in an unlivable situation."

It is a serious misrepresentation to believe that human beings can believe what is not in their best interest. The failure to recognize this has led to all manner of unhappiness and confounded some of our best minds. Dostoevsky famously thought that consciousness was a curse. Actually, only a cursed consciousness is cursed, and he only believed that because he unconsciously—and impossibly—believed it would enable him to become blessed. Seen in this context, what we are accustomed to calling *rational* and *irrational* has to be redefined. When science ridicules religion for being irrational, and when religion denounces science for overreaching, both worldviews are missing the point. One denies what the other affirms; yet both hold the beliefs they do because of how they define "the good life." And that can never be arrived at objectively.

Moreover, science, which has always been regarded as virtually interchangeable with the notion of rationality, has had their position of epistemic eminence seriously undermined. Many scientists no longer see scientific progress as the straightforward accumulation of one scientific truth after another. They see scientific truth making sense within paradigms– a paradigm being a conceptual frame of reference, a model that directs us as to how to observe and interpret events. Accordingly, anyone who takes the idea of paradigm shifts seriously, with due respect for science and its prodigious accomplishments, puts us under no obligation to embrace the traditional materialistic paradigm where all things are seen as reducible to matter. Highly intelligent human beings have thought otherwise. So nothing is preventing us from seeing the world paradigmatically as a living organism— the biosphere—or as a giant information-processing system where mind, not matter, is seen as the irreducible stuff of the universe, or as a divinely inspired creation, or as a cosmic accident without meaning or purpose.

A worldview, how ever skillfully reasoned, is never a settled issue, because every system of beliefs rests on the observed or proven truth of its paradigm. But paradigms are neither observable nor provable. Moreover, as mentioned earlier, the physics of quantum mechanics set limits as to what can even be reliably observed. Within the same decade of the quantum mechanics upheaval, another radical intellectual revolution took place in mathematics. Historically, mathematics, along with science, has been regarded as the most rational of human cognitive pursuits, but suddenly it also had to make room for faith. In 1931, Kurt Godel, probably the greatest logician since Aristotle, upended the dogma that to be true everything in mathematics could be proved. His *incompleteness theorem* proved mathematically that it was impossible. Now, if the most exacting and rigorous intellectual pursuers of knowledge—scientists and mathematicians—are forced to make assumptions that are neither observable nor provable, it ought to be evident that the proponents of any belief system will be forced to do likewise.

The failure to recognize the unavoidable presence of the subjective in what we come to believe has produced endlessly pointless debates. Believers argue with non-believers, advocates of positive thinking argue with proponents of negative thinking, because each fails to appreciate that the beliefs of the opposition are seen as equally positive. Lao Tsu rightly said, "The good man does not argue; he who argues is not good."

It follows that the person who knows that he or she *is* good would not argue with the personal beliefs of others, because they would know that all belief systems seek the good, how ever mistaken he thought they were. From time beyond memory, no one has ever embraced a belief system that was not seen as the best choice for a happier life, which paradoxically includes one that makes us unhappy. It is unfortunate that all cultures also support belief systems that extol unhappiness, that there is redemption in self-imposed suffering. That is what possibly led Freud to observe, "Happiness is no cultural value." In addition, "Where there is no friction, there is no growth … Anything worth having doesn't come easy … You have to feel worse before you feel better … Those things that hurt, also instruct," and "No pain, no gain" are the sort of cultural maxims praised in both religious and secular circles. Notice that these beliefs always have this means–ends characteristic.

Normally, we speak of the means in the means–ends relationship as an activity that, in itself, may not be especially pleasurable, but *causes* good ends. But that is not always the case. We may take up jogging because it is a means to cardiovascular health, but that doesn't preclude the possibility of running as an end in itself, going for what is known as the "runner's high." Writing a book may be the means to fame and fortune, but the craft of writing itself can become a pleasure in its own right. Not only may means become ends in themselves, ends may become means to still other ends. Orgasm is the best example: the means to a baby, as well as to intimacy with one's spouse, and an end in itself. You can say that in any order. Even happiness, which is the irreducible end of all means, may itself be the means to more happiness. It is well known that those who "radiate happiness" often attract others.

## Unhappiness–The Quintessential Contradiction

Despite these exceptions, most of the time the means is experienced as a necessary evil. That would certainly be the case with the maxims cited above. My ambition at this point is to obviate the distinction between means and ends altogether as it relates to happiness. The way to do that is to understand that when the end is clearly and unequivocally seen as good, the means by which to accomplish it would also be experienced as good. Any parent who has ever nursed a sick child never experiences the means that were necessary to make the child well as a struggle. Under those circumstances, we don't do anything because we ought to or even because we want to; we automatically do whatever it takes, and we do so without reservation. Walt Whitman captured the essence of this sentiment perfectly, "I give nothing as duties. What others give as duties, I give as living impulses." It follows that when we feel that great effort and sacrifice is required, we are either having second thoughts about the desirability of the enterprise or, more commonly, its feasibility. And the latter is always the case as it applies to negative self-reference.

Earlier I tried to show that the problem of negative self-reference is a paradox for which no solution is possible. Let's flesh out this idea further. To begin with, choosing to believe that we are bad or—in what amounts to the same thing—*choosing to feel bad* is manifestly an act of self-punishment. Freud, ever the astute observer, noted, "This need for punishment is the worst enemy of our therapeutic efforts." The key to understanding an emotion, then, is to be found in uncovering the rationale for punishment.

Consider the archetypal case—the slave driver and the slave. The slave driver whips the slave because he wants the slave to feel and do what he believes the slave would not willingly feel and do otherwise. He does this because he believes by getting the slave to conform, it will enable him to feel and do what he, the slave driver, wants. In effect, the slave driver wants the slave to feel bad, so that *he* may feel good. As disagreeable as that might be for the slave, his compliance is neither irrational nor self-defeating. The slave recognizes that to resist may end in greater physical harm and even death. Furthermore, circumstances may change and there is always the possibility of escape.

When the slave driver and the slave, the punisher and the punished, are one and the same person, significant differences and implications emerge, all of them contradictory and self-defeating. When punishment is unrelated to questions of life and limb, our metaphorical whip must be redefined in strictly psychological terms. But what is psychological punishment other than the experience of having been made to feel bad? If the punisher always wants the punished to feel bad, in order that *he* may feel good, then, perforce, the self-punisher engages in that activity for the same reason. How often have we heard or experienced *I know that feeling bad doesn't do any good but ...* The very existence of the disclaimer is the surest evidence that we always sensed that we were doing it to ourselves and that it indeed must aim at some good.

But even that much self-awareness never makes any difference, because it is incomplete. The good that it is intended to achieve is never spelled out. We never hear, for instance, *I feel bad in order to feel good* or *I believe that*

*I am bad in order to believe that I am good.* The self-deprecator resembles a child who finds himself in a dentist's chair kicking and screaming, oblivious of the intended benefits of dentistry and bewildered as to why he is sitting there in the first place. The self-deprecator is in a perpetual quandary, because he is only dimly aware of the purpose for which he has put himself down, and wastes his energies by focusing on what he mistakenly believes are the "causes" of his unhappiness. What compounds his dilemma is that even if he were aware that the fiction of there being something wrong with him has really been created to make something right with him, he will never achieve his objective. It will always be an unfinished business—an insoluble paradox. The reason is that, as regards negative self-reference, means–ends kind of thinking is always self-defeating. Why?

If we deny that there is something wrong with us—that we are good—that makes us bad (arrogant, conceited). If we accept that there is something wrong with us, that makes us good (modest, self-effacing). Now if we invented imperfection as a way of making us good, that can never happen because, as just stated, to believe that we are good makes us bad. In other words, to believe that that we are good makes us bad and to believe that we are bad makes us good. One affirms and the other denies but the outcome is the same—never ending self-deprecation. As long as feeling bad or believing we are bad is inextricably associated with feeling good or believing we are good, it follows that feeling good and believing that we are good must cancel themselves out if we want to continue to feel good and to be good. It's a Catch-22 of the highest and deepest order.

If unhappiness has never been fully described and understood, it is due entirely to the failure to appreciate that its cause was not to be found in our viscera, our genes, our biochemistry, our brains, or our environments, nor was it the result of evil, foolishness, injustice, or human perversity. Unhappiness always was and always will be a paradox, an inadvertent self-imposed double bind that answers the question that prompted the writing of this book: *What are you afraid would happen if you were not unhappy?* The answer is *I would be more unhappy*, an idea that would have to qualify as the profoundest absurdity ever contrived by the human mind.

Although it is always an adventure trying to puzzle out what Samuel Beckett, the existential playwright, has written, when he says in *Endgame*, "Nothing is funnier than unhappiness," one senses that that exquisitely honed absurdist mind was undeniably on to something. To put it in the most banal of terms, unhappiness is an impossible attempt at self-improvement.

Diagrammatically, it would look like this:

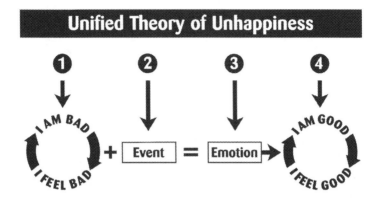

As we can see, I have revised the sequence of events. As in all theories of emotion the explanation is believed to start with an environmental event– what William James called "the exciting fact." That is not the place to begin nor does it even start with the percipient, but with what resides dormant in the head of all of us—self-doubt. It is this amorphous feeling state, this hovering dispositional readiness that enables us to experience the entire repertoire of nameable emotions. This impossible state of mind  what Thoreau might have been referring to this when he said that most people "live lives of quiet desperation" or what Freud might have sensed when he spoke of our "everyday unhappiness" and what I earlier characterized as the "ignorance of the average." George Eliot, in her novel *Middlemarch,* described it more adroitly when she spoke of that "unhappy consciousness ... the minute processes which prepare human misery ... that delicate poise and transition that leads to mania, crime, and insanity."

Although a few authors have correctly pointed out that emotions are in some way the result of choice, most people are only partially convinced, because it doesn't seem entirely in accord with their experience. While there is often an inchoate sense that we are contributing in some ill defined way to an emotional reaction, the emotion still doesn't seem altogether a matter of choice. The reason for this is that normal human emotionality, as we have come to know it, was prefigured early on—at that moment in our self-reflective history when human beings first accepted that they were flawed. This belief became the preparatory mindset for which the actual events of the world become the triggers. So when the events come into play, the specific emotion appears to have been caused by them, when in fact, the emotion was only catalyzed by the preexisting belief that we are not good.

Socrates said, "Virtue is knowledge of the good. He who knows the good chooses the good." He might have more accurately said that *virtue is the knowledge that one is good*, and *he who knows he is good necessarily chooses the good*. Earlier in this book, I quoted the Socratic dictum—"The unexamined life is not worth living." Surely, he was unaware of the insoluble nature of his program. What became the philosophic centerpiece for all the centuries of introspection that followed never doubted that the examiner was flawed, would always be, and that his greatness lay in the recognition of this self-reflective uncertainty. Rather than being the solution to the problem of unhappiness, it was a credo that unwittingly became its creation. In effect, unhappiness is a strategy we invented to protect ourselves against what was never wrong with ourselves in the first place

Saint Augustine said, "Love God and do as you please." Anyone who can love God is only fully able do so because self-doubt has been removed from his reflections. This is not done by realizing our potential or striving for excellence. Human excellence refers to achievement and is never attained by reaching for some will-o-the-wisp end game. Its attainment is the by-product of loving what we do. Similarly, what it means to be a person is not an achievement. Our humanity, uncontaminated by self-doubt, naturally predisposes us to love. When someone with that mindset does as he pleases, would demeaning another human being even rise up as a temptation?

All the behavior that follows is keyed to that starting note. If we really loved ourselves, (more simply, just didn't hate ourselves) would it even be possible to hate others? What would we have to realize or strive for to become more worthwhile in our hearts? Can we become more human than we were yesterday? Were we ever not worth loving? Weren't we always children of God?

## Dissolving Unhappiness

For those who are getting uncomfortable with all this talk of God, don't be alarmed. I am not reneging on the original intention of this book, which is to provide a strictly earth–based, psychological explanation of unhappiness. For me, the existence of a sensibility that allows us to take genuine pleasure in the happiness of another is the most compelling argument for a divine presence, because there is no palpable reason why empathy and compassion should have emerged from our prebiotic soup and ultimately appear in the human psyche. The sensibility that I am describing ought not be confused with what others might call moral sensibility and its preoccupation with right and wrong. Nor is it what evolutionary psychologists call reciprocal altruism, whose evolutionary claim is that mutual cooperation augments survival. The mindset that I am alluding to is motivated neither by guilt nor survival. Perhaps the clearest manifestation of it is anonymous giving—a sensibility whose greatest pleasure is indistinguishable from the recipient's pleasure. So whether "love God and do as you please" is experienced as deeply felt religious truth, or an allegorical account of human goodness, the gratitude and kindness that it inspires is what lies at the heart of self-acceptance and inner peace.

Any psychology that fails to recognize that unhappiness is reducible to the belief that there is something wrong with us and does not recognize, at the outset, the irreconcilability of a consciousness that condemns itself will never fully succeed. Human consciousness can be raised, altered, analyzed, shocked, confronted, medicated, hypnotized, and even lobotomized. We can go through recovery gain any number of insights but, in the end, all their systems of interlocking beliefs, practices, and therapies are merely antidotal. The only way to settle this problem is to cut off, right at the start, any assumption that we are defective. We cannot negatively refer to ourselves and avoid this felt contradiction, this cognitive dissonance. If the goal of therapy is to raise consciousness, not putting ourselves down is the starting point. Then, consciousness will have been raised in every way that matters.

If the quest of psychology has been to specify the conditions under which happiness is possible, then it is now possible to state unreservedly that *no such conditions exist.* If unhappiness is reducible to the single belief that we are flawed, under what conditions could that choice be rendered impossible? It would be as pointless to try to specify the conditions under which we come to believe in justice or democracy. If we were asked how we came to believe in either, would we specify the conditions that caused us to believe, or would we simply state our faith? Our view of the world and how we see ourselves in it is not decided by argument and evidence; these only support what we are prepared to believe. But *what we are prepared to believe is limited by our inability to choose what we don't believe to be in our best interest.* The discerning reader may have noticed that this premise infiltrates the entire book. And since an explanation is only as secure as its starting assumption, it matters that we see this belief about beliefs, this meta-belief, if you will, as incontrovertible.

Socrates correctly believed that a teacher doesn't really teach the student anything new. He or she is more like a midwife who assists the students in rearranging what they are already hard-wired to know. Borrowing a phrase from Noam Chomsky in a different context, there is a "deep structure" in the brain that informs us how we came to hold our beliefs and, specifically, how they have been unavoidably motivated by its "good aspect." This can be directly confirmed by introspection. When faced with alternatives, is it humanly possible to choose what we believe to be what is not in our best interest—the worst of two alternatives? Were we to say that it is, how ever we choose to explain our denial, would that be possible unless we also believed it was in our best interest to do so?

Blaise Pascal, a great soul and one of the finest minds of the seventeenth century, believed that happiness consists in being able to sit peacefully in a room by one's self. Most of us have had momentary glimpses of intense happiness, sometimes because of a momentous event and at other times for no obvious reason. Did we become happy because we used the moment to remind us that there is nothing wrong with us, or did the fact that we stop believing that there was something wrong with us allow the moment to make us happy? In either case, as long as we are not putting ourselves down, where we happen to find ourselves does not determine our happiness. It may be that the future is uncertain, but we who reflect on it need not be.

# Dissolutions–Excerpts and Extrapolations

Some of you may have found the material hefty enough so as to require further thought. This last section is designed to provide you with a capsule version of most of the ideas found throughout the book. The terseness of the approach is intended to make it easier to locate the fictions that may have led to and sustained your unhappiness, and a briefly stated dissolution that I hope will settle any lingering questions that you may still have had.

**Fiction**: The goal of therapy is to raise consciousness.
**Dissolution**: Start by not putting yourself down, and your consciousness will have been raised in every way that matters.

**Fiction**: Learning how to cope is the touchstone of successful therapy.
**Dissolution**: Learning how to cope can only happen when we start to feel better about what troubles us. The interesting question is why only better and not good? Isn't that because better is perceived as good, but good is not perceived as better?

**Fiction**: Pride is either a virtue or a sin.
**Dissolution**: Neither. If we didn't define ourselves as bad, the issue wouldn't even exist.

**Fiction**: Letting it all hang out is good therapy.
**Dissolution**: Or it is the folly of confounding self-expression with self-knowledge.

**Fiction:** What we learned to believe in the past enabled us to be unhappy in the present.

**Dissolution:** That is only half the story. What we learned was originally designed to do the opposite. It was learned at that earlier time to protect us from that future which has now become the present.

**Fiction:** We can't know happiness unless we have known unhappiness.

**Dissolution:** That is as preposterous as saying that we can never enjoy sight unless we have been blind, or benefitted from breathing unless you have gasped for air. Anyone who makes such a statement doesn't really understand why he or she needs to be unhappy.

**Fiction:** We are free to choose.

**Dissolution:** Not entirely. All our choices are limited by our inability to choose what we don't believe is in our best interest.

**Fiction:** Criminals are either sick or evil.

**Dissolution:** Neither. They are unhappy and dangerous.

**Fiction:** Language is finite; it can never fully express what is really going on inside us.

**Dissolution:** Language may never express everything that is going on inside us, but it is perfectly suited to account for our unhappiness. Language is not at fault because we are not at fault.

**Fiction:** Identity issues are a major problem in contemporary life.

**Dissolution:** If we felt free to do what we really wanted, would we know who we were? If we were happy, would identity be an issue?

**Fiction:** To err is human, to forgive divine.

**Dissolution:** To err is human, to forgive unnecessary.

**Fiction:** Change is difficult because habits are hard to break.

**Dissolution:** Change only appears difficult because we have not really decided to change. We are only saying that we *should* change, which is to say that we are not entirely convinced of the advantages of altering our behavior. For example, if we knew with absolute certainty that one more cigarette would cause our death, do we think our urges would continue to be "irresistible?"

**Fiction**: You should have known better.

**Dissolution**: This is a genuinely mindless statement, because people are being blamed for not being prescient. Nobody plans on making mistakes, which means that people always automatically do their best; i.e., they act consistently with what they think is necessary to get what they want or don't want. But they are only guessing. When things don't turn out, we conclude that we didn't do our best, instead of recognizing that life is a horse race. "You should have known better" can be understood in one of two ways: either you are inherently not good enough, or in spite of your efforts, things didn't turn out. Insisting on the first interpretation is an error borne of the illusion that it will prod you to do better. Accepting the latter will allow you to be more enterprising, because it eliminates the fear of failure.

**Fiction**: Life is filled with contradictions.

**Dissolution**: Nature doesn't produce contradictions. It only appears that way because we make mistaken assumptions about nature that we're not aware of when we look at it. Psychologically speaking, the same is true when we look at ourselves who are also part of nature. The assumption is: I will be bad if I feel good or I will be good if I feel bad.

**Fiction**: Certain negative emotions states are basically healthy, benign, and adaptive.

**Dissolution**: A secular variation of suffering is good for the soul without the benefits of getting into heaven. It is an example of trying to convert mud into chocolate. When we don't know how to get rid of something, we often try to find a good use for it. So from all quarters we are instructed as to value of misery.

**Fiction**: My problem is that I'm a perfectionist.

**Dissolution**: The real problem is that, in believing that, we hope to *become* perfect. Stop believing that there is something wrong with you. If you find yourself resisting, think about this: isn't that a way of becoming perfect?

**Fiction**: The way to break an undesirable habit is to become disgusted with oneself.

**Dissolution**: Never start that way, because if we validate self-contempt as a method of breaking a habit, we will rarely succeed. Even when we do, we have to use the same method to maintain it. Disgust is unsustainable, and that is why there is so much recidivism.

**Fiction**: Delaying gratification requires discipline.

**Dissolution**: Not really. Delaying gratification is an effortless choice that occurs when it is absolutely clear that deferring present rewards will pay off more handsomely later on.

**Fiction**: Tolerance and open-mindedness are keys to happiness.

**Dissolution** There is a Yiddish saying: *It's good to be open-minded, but if you are too open-minded, your brains fall out.* Being open-minded about everything is not necessarily beneficial. It opens us up to everything that ails us. Are we open to the possibility of delighting in murder, of being incapable of loving, or of being genetically evil? Watch it; we may be open to being called dogmatic. Do we care?

**Fiction**: Not getting what we want makes us unhappy.

**Dissolution**: Not getting what we want makes an unhappy person unhappy. It makes a happy person only inconvenienced.

**Fiction**: Saint Francis said, "Blessed is he who expects nothing, for he shall never be disappointed."

**Dissolution**: With due respect to Francis, the statement might be improved as, "Blessed is he who expects everything; he will enjoy everything even more if he knows that he need not be disappointed if he does not get what he expects." But then again, Francis might have meant the same thing.

**Fiction**: We want things because they are good, and we feel bad when we don't get them.

**Dissolution**: On the contrary, things are good because we want them; and we feel bad when we don't get them, because we believe that *we* are not good.

**Fiction**: Greed is good.

**Dissolution**: A prime example of doublethink. Anyone who says that is already uncomfortable with his motives. Money divorced from ego can never be motivated by greed. Making money need not involve a guilty conscience. Decide that making money is good, or what amounts to the same thing, that you are good. Then the motive for making money will be restored to why it was invented in the first place—as a medium of exchange whose purpose was to buy goods and services, not for self-esteem.

**Fiction**: Jealousy will always exist to some degree. The trick is not to be overwhelmed by it.

**Dissolution**: That translates into *I need to believe I am inadequate and I have no idea as to why I am that way or how to change.*

**Fiction**: Bodily feelings have a logic of their own.

**Dissolution**: Actually, bodily feelings are non-specific stress reactions. They take on meaning only when we believed something before we got them.

**Fiction**: We have a right to be ourselves, to become the person we want to be, to feel what we feel, to be angry, upset, disappointed, etc.

**Dissolution**: Rights are legal concepts and have no place in psychology. We must stop trying to undo our unhappiness by appealing to our so-called rights. No one as ever been helped by such useless advice, which only tells us that we are not bad for being unhappy while failing to explain why we needed to feel bad in the first place.

**Fiction**: Body language is a useful tool for determining how we appear to others.

**Dissolution**: Only to one who is self-conscious. To someone who is not, one's external behavior is routinely graceful. Isn't that what we see when we say that someone is charismatic? Did Jesus or Buddha ever concern themselves with such matters?

**Fiction**: Depression may be the result of a chemical imbalance.

**Dissolution**: Depression always entails low self-esteem. In effect, biochemists are claiming that it is possible to synthesize a chemical that will transform self-hate into self-love. Twenty five hundred years have elapsed since the Greeks first tried their hand at love potions, and the promise still persists from modern psychopharmacology. How can we think love, whatever its object—self, God, family, spouse, nature, art, or country—is achievable via a psychoactive drug? What will we do until it is discovered?

**Fiction**: Emotions are evolutionarily adaptive reactions to environmental threats.

**Dissolution**: Evolution is a seductive theory, because survival seems to account for much of our behavior. But then there is unhappiness and suicide. What do these have to do with survival?

**Fiction**: People and events can be boring.

**Dissolution**: It is never the responsibility of the world that our interest be engaged. Boredom only occurs when we are afraid to retreat from what fails to interest us—and when we believe that we would not have what it takes to entertain ourselves if we did.

**Fiction**: I love you, but I don't like you.

**Dissolution**: Anyone who feels compelled to make that distinction invariably does so because they either feel responsible in some way for the behavior they observe or that they are bad for noticing it. Neither is true. We need not trick ourselves into believing that people are not defined by their behavior, because it makes us look and feel like liars, and it induces the other not to change.

**Fiction**: A loving mother ought to protect her children from disappointment.

**Dissolution**: A loving mother would do infinitely better to teach her children that they don't have to make themselves feel disappointed in order to get what they want. But that would only be possible if she learned that for herself.

**Fiction**: The child is father to the man.

**Dissolution**: In terms of his emotional life, the only history worth noting is the defining moment in which the child accepted the belief that he or she was bad. That prefigures all future unhappiness. And since that belief is taught everywhere in the culture, the *where* or *when* of history becomes irrelevant. Only the *why* matters—why did they accept the belief that they were bad? And that can be spelled out: to be accepted as good.

**Fiction**: People become anxious about not being self-confident.

**Dissolution**: Actually, anxiety and lack of self-confidence are the same thing. It is the feeling produced by believing that we won't be able to handle what may or *will* happen. It is never true. Aren't we still here?

**Fiction**: Beliefs are held because they are taught to us by others in our past.

**Dissolution**: Beliefs are not held because they are taught by others in the past. We learned them because we thought they were useful for our future. How else can we explain why we don't believe or retain everything that we were taught?

**Fiction**: Many of the events of the world are innately disturbing.

**Dissolution**: Before Galileo, Aristotle taught that things fell at different rates of speed, because it was believed that things were innately heavier than others. For over four hundred years, physicists no longer speak of things as having the essence of "heaviness." Why is it that the general population and most professionals are still Aristotelian? Why is it that they still speak of essences, of things being "innately disturbing?"

**Fiction**: We often do things that are bad for us.

**Dissolution**: We never believe that at the time we do it. It only appears that way when things don't turn out, because we started off believing that there is something wrong with us.

**Fiction**: Dostoevsky said that consciousness is a curse.

**Dissolution**: Actually, only a cursed consciousness is a curse. And he only believed that because he unconsciously—and impossibly—believed that would enable him to become blessed.

**Fiction**: The way to deal with fear is to directly confront it and learn to control it.

**Dissolution**: The way to deal with fear is to stop treating it as if it were an "it." We don't control a phantasm; we uncover the reason we invented it and make it fade away.

**Fiction**: Life is fundamentally tragic. When we accept that, we transcend it.

**Dissolution**: When we deny that, we dissolve it.

**Fiction**: People often act in ways that they don't believe.

**Dissolution**: That is never the case. It is impossible to act inconsistently with what one believes. If it appears that way, we really don't believe what we say we believe but would feel worse if we admitted it.

**Fiction**: When people insist on seeing the glass as half empty as opposed to half full, that is the result of negative thinking.

**Dissolution**: *Negative thinking* is a misnomer that misses the point. People who think that way do so for two reasons: as a way of preventing the glass from becoming totally empty and as a way of filling it up.

**Fiction**: Different therapeutic approaches are useful.

**Dissolution**: Since anything can be said to be the cause of unhappiness, it follows that anything can be therapeutic. When we are ready to stop what we earlier decided to start, anything can be said to have "worked."

**Fiction**: In order to be happy, we must give up our desire for unconditional love.

**Dissolution**: In order to be happy, we must know that we are unconditionally lovable. If we do not let ourselves know that, we mistakenly believe that by making ourselves needy that is way we are going to get their love. It's not, and even if we did get it, there will never be enough of it.

**Fiction**: Emotional problems are caused by the subtle interaction among genetic, cultural, biochemical, and environmental factors.

**Dissolution**: This ubiquitous, academic content-free statement is both irrefutable and barren. Where in human affairs might this assertion not apply? Will such a statement ever be remotely useful to anyone who is emotionally troubled?

**Fiction**: The purpose of life is to realize our potential.

**Dissolution**: If life is said to have any purpose, it is to be happy. And that will never be accomplished by realizing our potential. Will we become more worth loving tomorrow than we are today? Will we become more human than we were yesterday? Were we ever not worth loving? Weren't we always children of God?

**Fiction**: The pursuit of happiness requires effort and entails risks.

**Dissolution**: On the contrary, it is unhappiness that requires effort, which is aimed at eliminating risk. But risk, in psychological terms, is ultimately reducible to the fear of being unhappy. It follows that if happiness were risky, that would mean that happiness could lead to unhappiness—the profoundest of absurdities.

**Fiction**: Why do bad things happen to good people?

**Dissolution**: From a psychological point of view, anybody who really believed that they were good would not even ask that question, because they would never suspect that they were being singled out by God or Fate for some special punishment. For anyone who knew that they were good, the paranoid exclamation, "Why me?" would be instantly answered, "Why anybody?" And even if we insisted that we were being singled out, what's preventing us from seeing it as an opportunity?

**Fiction**: Caring means feeling bad when the other is feeling bad.

**Dissolution**: It is this unconscious and therefore unchallenged belief that has done more than any other to undermine a happy relationship, because it underwrites unhappiness as a precondition of love. One has no necessary connection with the other. The remedy is to love the other person enough to let them feel bad *without* feeling bad yourself. In this way, we end up not resenting them, and it also might help them to stop feeling bad.

**Fiction**: Everyone needs to be loved.

**Dissolution**: Only if we need proof that we are worth loving. If we have no beliefs to the contrary, it frees us to do what we were really born to do—to love, which is more enjoyable anyway, If we can get the ones we love to know what we know, we *will* get it back—not because we need it, but because we are giving them an opportunity to do what they were also born to do–to love.

**Fiction**: It is important to be able to recognize manipulative people.

**Dissolution**: No, it's not. To be manipulated means to be made to do what we don't want to do. If we know that we are not bad for saying no and also that they don't have to feel bad if we do, then how can they make us do what we don't want to do?

**Fiction**: We ought not be judgmental.

**Dissolution**: That advice becomes unnecessary when we understand that we only call others bad because we think that will make us better, and they proceed to feel bad because they think likewise.

**Fiction**: Everyone fears rejection.

**Dissolution**: It is not rejection that we fear but the possibility that the rejecter may be right in their assessment of us. We don't need to waste our time thinking about what other people believe about us; they are only mirrors. We might ask ourselves, instead, is it really possible that we are preventing the other from accepting us? Happily, the answer will always be no, because it turns out that we don't have that power.

**Fiction**: You always hurt the one you love.

**Dissolution**: Only if we believe that their feeling hurt is the test of their loving us. And that only matters because we suspect our own value.

**Fiction**: It's good to be afraid.

**Dissolution**: Why? Are we so stupid so as not to know what to do if we weren't?

**Fiction**: Psychology should move away from *feeling* good and toward the idea of *doing* good.

**Dissolution**: Feeling good can only happen *if we know we are good*. Feeling good and doing good are inextricably connected.

# Bibliography

*Diagnostic and Statistical Manual of Mental Disorders,* 4th ed. Washington, DC: American Psychiatric Assn., 1994.

Davis, Paul, and John Gribben. *The Matter Myth.* New York: Simon and Schuster, 1991.

Eccles, Sir John et al., *Nobel Prize Conversations.* Dallas, TX: Saybrook Publishing Co., 1985.

Frankl, Viktor. *Man's Search For Meaning.* New York: Washington Square Press, 1984.

Freud, Sigmund. *New Introductory Lectures on Psychoanalysis.* New York: W. W. Norton & Co., 1933.

Freud, Sigmund. *Civilization and Its Discontents.* New York: Doubleday & Co., 1958.

———. *Beyond the Pleasure Principle.* New York: Bantam Books, 1959.

Gazzaniga, Michael S. *The Social Brain.* New York: Basic Books, 1985.

Horgan, John. *Undiscovered Mind.* Free Press, 1999.

James, W., and C. G Lange. *The Emotions.* Baltimore: William & Wilkins Co., 1922.

James, William. *The Varieties of Religious Experience.* New York: Collier Books, 1961.

Kagan, Jerome. *The Nature of the Child.* New York: Basic Books, 1986.

———. *Galen's Prophecy.* New York: Basic Books, 1994.

Maslow, Abraham H. *Motivation and Personality.* New York: Harper and Row, 1970.

———. *Toward a Psychology of Being.* Van Nostrand Reinhold, 1968.

Pascal, Blaise. *Pensees.* New York: E. P. Dutton & Company, 1958.

Paton, H. J. *Immanuel Kant: Critique of Practical Reason and Other Writings in Moral Philosophy.* (Translated and edited by White Beck Lewis. Chicago: University of Chicago Press, 1949). *Philosophy* 26 (1951): 176–178.

Penrose, Roger. *The Emperor's New Mind.* Oxford, England: Oxford University Press, 1989.

Popper, Karl, and John Eccles. *The Self and Its Brain*. Berlin: Springer Verlag, 1977.

Schachter, Stanley. *Feelings and Emotions*. New York: Academic Press, 1970.

Selye, Hans. *Stress Without Distress*. New York: New American Library, 1974.

Selye, Hans. *The Stress of Life*. New York: McGraw-Hill, 1976.

Skinner, B. F. *About Behaviorism*. New York: Vintage Books, 1974.

Stevenson, Leslie. *Seven Theories of Human Nature*. Oxford, England: Oxford University Press, 1974.

Vaihinger, Hans. *The Philosophy of "As If."* Translated by C. K. Ogden. New York: Harcourt, Brace & Co.,1925.

Wilson, E. O. *Sociobiology: The New Synthesis*. Cambridge, MA: Belknap Press of Harvard University Press, 1975.

Wittgenstein, Ludwig. *Tractatus Logico-Philosophicus*. London: Routledge & Keegan, 1922.

———. *Philosophical Investigations*. Translated by G. E. M. Anscombe. Oxford: Basil Blackwell, 1953.

Wright, Richard. *The Moral Animal*. New York: New York: Vintage Books, 1995.

Direct inquiries may be made to Peter Spinogatti:
Telephone: 631 424-0202
www.dissolvingunhappiness.com
www.explainingunhapipiness.com
Email: peterspinogatti@yahoo.com
Explainingunhappiness.blogspot.com